YO(
COVID-19 & THE CABAL

Peter Tremblay

Foreword by Dr. John Chang

Agora Books

Agora Books™
Ottawa, Canada

Agora Books
P.O. Box 24191
300 Eagleson Road
Kanata, Ontario K2M 2C3

Agora Books is a self-publishing agency for authors that was launched by The Agora Cosmopolitan which is a registered not-for-profit corporation.

ISBN 978-1-77838-001-3

Printed in Canada

Book cover artwork by Agora Publishing.

Contents

FOREWORD

I'M GOING TO TELL YOU something that you won't find in the text books of medical schools. Aliens not only exist, but a variety of them have been in contact with humans, including those in business. With that said, let's say some of those contacts reportedly have not been with the best of intentions.

Dr. Roger Lier was an American surgeon who became known for removing highly advanced implants, nanotechnology microchips imbedded by some of the more demonic aliens. But why go through the inefficient work of abducting humans, one-by-one for various medical experiments, when you can contrive mass fear in tandem with greedy and megalomaniac ultra-insiders only too willing to sell-out the human race during a so-called pandemic for the sole purpose of coercing everyone into injecting themselves with invasive nanotechnology?

Dr. Maree Batchelor, MD, who worked in mainstream medicine as a GP (family doctor) for over twenty years, has been a trailblazer in the medical community for exposing the alien nanotechnology, similar to that being applied in the jab, used against her patients by ultra-insiders and regressive entities to enslave humanity. This technology includes implants used to monitor human subjects and to repress our evolution into a higher dimensional consciousness. Indeed, the jab has nothing to do with protecting "public health," and everything to do with the pursuit of a New World Order where free will no longer exists.

To expedite a New World Order, the shadow that manages Google has been seeking to "sanitize" their search engine of any critical information that conflicts with the agenda of a cabal. Google has therefore "sanitized" YouTube, removing any interviews, like those featured in this book, that expose a nefarious Archonic agenda against humanity.

Some of my earnest colleagues in the medical community are facing punishment for providing COVID-19 prevention and life-saving early treatment, for sharing information on the dangers of the COVID-19 so-called vaccine, and for telling us that we need to wake up and smell the coffee. To borrow a quote from the *Wizard of Oz*, "we're not in Kansas anymore." Yet, The Ontario College of Physicians and Surgeons is one of many authoritative organizations that has sold out doctors and humanity in general in a bid to appease its evil puppet masters.

It is doubtful that aliens have been abducting humans under the noses of ultra-insiders to have tea and scones and with them. It is also apparent that with every injection of the fake vaccine people take, they are enabling a cabal to essentially play God over their body. The Cabal wants to control who lives and who dies, and they are prepared to create whatever fiction necessary to support their agenda.

The Canadian Broadcasting Corporation's (CBC) use of a photo of a mannequin to represent an ICU patient in an October 2, 2021 report is a microcosm of the layers of deception and manipulation used in the effort to produce fear in the public, to corral the masses and make them rush into taking the jab. If there are no patients around, presto, just bring in mannequins, reinforced by other fake data that can be shown on the daily news.

David Icke further suggests that the aim of "the jab" is to surreptitiously sterilize all recipients and then offer artificial pro-creation reminiscent of Aldous Huxley's *Brave New World* (1932), as the solution to the problem, whereby anyone who does seek to procreate must apply to those in power for an undoubtedly expensive permit. This cabal believes that there are just too many people on Earth, so controlling Earth's future population this way is the "right thing to do." Their rank-and-file have spawned eugenics movements and spin-off organizations, which often seek to conceal themselves as "family planning" or "environ-mental" groups concerned with "overpopulation" along with CO_2 emissions from "global warning." And, if you think this is silly, just ask experts like Dr. Suzie Basile, who documents the continued practice of clandestine sterilization of First Nations women. Women all over the world have likewise been subjected to such sterilization. This mass-injection is more of the same, but on a bigger scale, with all human beings on Earth as the target of eugenics.

Dr. Carrie Madej's reports with horror that she and her col-leagues discovered a self-aware artificial life form that sprouted tentacles resulting from the interactions of nanotechnology in the mRNA jab; this is the calling card of collusion between alien entities and the ultra-insiders who have sought to conceal their presence as simply the rantings of so-called conspiracy theorists. Reportedly, what Dr. Madej discovered was "hydra Linnaeus," a synthetic versions of the hydra vulgaris, which is found in nature.

I know for a fact that these aliens in the guise of humans have been infiltrating institutions for years because I have seen their presence. People who label me as some sort of conspiracy theorist don't impress me. My duty in the field of medicine implores me to serve my patients, and to serve humanity in the process, with honour and integrity. If I see it's a duck, I will say it's a duck, and I won't call it a cat in order to serve some ideological predispositions.

Aliens are all around us. Some are also reportedly underground. The apparent objective of the oppressive ones are to control, enslave, and assimilate. David Icke further points out that anyone who elects to resist their agenda is being subjected to gaslighting, mass deception, censorship, and, shockingly, the projection of invasive EMF delivered messages of "bliss" about the jabs right into the heads of people who have sought to resist in order to mind control them to get it.

Dr. Scott Corder, who is a well-respected family physician in the state of Kansas, sought to warn humanity about the extraterrestrial threat. The COVID-19 "vaccine" and the fascism that has accompanied it, with the strategic support of YouTube, shows us that the threat was definitely not the figment of his imagination.

As a member of the medical community, I believe that I have the experience to know the normal bio-physical attributes of a human being. Having seen and met some of these public heath authority zombies conveying their programmed instructions to us all, let's just say I have some doubts about some of these entities.

In an interview entitled "Retired US Army Commander Bob Dean Confirms Interaction with Extraterrestrials," the experiences of Robert Dean, who was trained as an intelligence analyst and became a command sergeant major when he served in the U.S. Army, is documented. When he arrived at Paris, France in the summer of 1963, his top-secret clearance was upgraded to a level called "Cosmic Top-Secret," the highest level of security classification in NATO. He remarked that one of the humanoid alien groups he met was totally human, like us.

"They could sit next to you in a theatre or restaurant, or an airplane, or a bus—it doesn't matter. They could be in your midst and you'd never know. Good God, they could be everywhere. Well, we were to find over the years that they are pretty much everywhere. They are in our midst. When I retired in 1976, we learned that there were at least a dozen more from different places."

Various public health authorities have been inserted in their positions over many years of meticulous planning to do the job of leading us to this *plandemic*; and it's certainly not in service of humanity. They are one head of the Medusa, of a mind that is responsible for coordinating a *plandemic* narrative, which includes making sure responsible doctors and nurses are repressed in saving fellow earthbound humans from what our scientific data reveals, data you won't find on YouTube.

When Dr. Peter McCullough says that COVID-19 "vaccines" are agents of bioterrorism, he's absolutely right. And, for speaking the truth, an eminent physician and other brave physicians have been banned by YouTube, a principal agent of this agenda. When Dr. Roger Hodkinson, a critically acclaimed Canadian physician, refers in the following pages to the oppression of basic medical knowledge on the normal way of dealing with a coronavirus through herd immunity in favour of an effort to whip-up conditions to take the jab, he also speaks the truth. When Nobel Laureate Dr. Luc Montagnier sounds the alarm bells about the ticking time bomb of human-body-destroying artificial genetics now targeted against children, who have naturally robust immunities to coronaviruses, he also speaks the truth.

It is my opinion that humanity's only hope is to begin to understand that the COVID-19 *plandemic* is an invasion wave planned by a consortium of manipulative aliens to use the jab to pacify the human population via artificial intelligence, all in their efforts to seize control of our planet. I wish this was not true, but it is what the evidence suggests. With that said, I hope that one day very soon, more of my fellow humans will realize that our immediate challenge is not a threat from COVID-19, with "vaccines" as our only "saviour," but instead a psychopathic ultra-insider-endorsed manipulative alien agenda that has taken hypnotic hold over the planet.

I wish you Godspeed my fellow human beings.

—John Chang, M.D., Ph.D.

INTRODUCTION

COVID-19 AND THE SO-CALLED VACCINE are the latest manifestations of a crypto-Nazi mind that was let loose after World War II to infiltrate and wreak havoc across the globe. YouTube colludes in hiding the truth from public eyes as part of an Orwellian apparatus to expedite a global totalitarian society run by technocrats and the military with the same demonic agenda that inspired the Nazi takeover of Germany and much of Europe.

This book features transcripts of interviews with Canadian doctors and others whose testimony was deleted by YouTube. This includes the testimony of Dr. Francis Christian (Appendix 1), who was intrigued at how the prevailing climate of censorship against world renowned physicians is so remarkably similar to the censorship that accompanied the rise of Nazi Germany. Well, that's because the same clique that led the Nazis used the intervening time since their supposed defeat to regroup themselves in an effort to complete their goal of a Fourth Reich; this "pandemic" is only their latest attempt.

The truth of the matter is that the Nazis never really lost World War II. Their presumed defeat was a complete charade, and now the evil force that manipulated Germans to supporting the rise of Adolf Hilter is trying to use the same playbook

If you rely on your schooling for your appreciation of World War II, this will appear to be crazy talk. Ha, ha, ha. The Nazis were defeated, the Allies prevailed, and democracy won, right? Actually wrong. You must not have heard of Operation Paperclip in 1945 and the Battle of Antarctica in 1947. The world that you think you live in is the world "they" want you to live in.

It is apparent that the same people who seek to conceal the testimony of this book and the testimony of so many others who have sought to present the truth about COVID-19 and "vaccines" are of the same mind as those who perpetrated destruction and death in the rise of Nazi Germany.

The chief medical "expert" of Nazi Germany was Dr. Joseph Mengele, a leading perpetrator of the Holocaust and its inhumane and fatal medical experiments on Jewish people and others. It therefore comes as no surprise that a supposed pandemic run by a cabal of Nazis would demand that people be required by law to receive injections with verifiably toxic agents of an "experimental" vaccine with links to injuries and death. All this with no liability at all to the manufacturers of the injections.

In Germany during the 1930s, the Nazis infiltrated the police, the education system, the justice system, and the whole medical system, and it was their doctors who were appointed as experts to preside over medical experiments involving euthanasia. Similarly, people needlessly died from "COVID-19" as a result of having been denied the care they needed because their deaths were needed to justify the calls to "vaccinate" everyone.

There are doctors and their patients who recovered from COVID-19 within just a couple of days after having taken high dose of Vitamins C and D. But, we can't show that now can we,

YouTube police? Delete! Delete! Saving lives like that would make people recover from the COVID-19 system, and that would result in people turning to vitamins instead of our gene therapy device... I mean "vaccine." We need to deprive people of safe solutions to treating COVID-19 and show as many people as we can on YouTube and cable TV news dying in emergency rooms so they will cry out for our mRNA "vaccination" program.

All the "old people," minorities, and other "undesirables" were also "euthanized" in Nazi Germany, with the doctors and other medical staff being instructed to lie about the circumstances of their death in the same way that today's doctors are being coerced, as evidenced in the pages that follow.

YouTube's role in all of this has been to deny those doctors and medical staff the opportunity of presenting the facts of their persecution in defence of democracy and against a tyranny that today's Nazis seek to rekindle.

Thanks to Operation Paperclip in 1945, and willing participants who have sold their soul to a demonic agenda, a crypto-Nazi ego is now running our world to the ground from the shadows, hiding behind a dwindling face of democratic pretensions.

YouTube is a manifestation of such an ego, and it is able to operate outside the reach of the very institutions and norms designed to affirm a culture of democracy.

Operation Paperclip was an American sponsored program in which more than 1,600 German scientists, engineers, and technicians were actively recruited from Nazi Germany to the U.S. for government employment after the end of World War II, between 1945 and 1959. It is furthermore notable that Adolf Hitler's actual body was also never found.

Where we are today is the result of a collective failure to pursue critical knowledge and to learn the lessons of the past.

Societies that fail to learn the lessons of an authentic history are doomed to repeat it. It is sad, therefore, that it appears that we are operating in ignorance of an obvious effort to subjugate the human population to evil medical experiments for commercial profit.

The result of Operation Paperclip was that crypto-Nazis and their sympathizers in big business have been able to systematically direct our planet Earth from the shadows into a spiralling dystopia.

In the article "Did US Navy battle UFOs protecting Nazi Antarctic sanctuary in 1947?" Dr. Michael Salla cites intelligence reports of a U.S. Naval expedition that went to Antarctica under Admiral Richard Byrd to try to stamp out Nazis who were reportedly stationed there.

Originally scheduled for a six-month period, the "scientific" expedition was officially called "The United States Navy Antarctic Development Program," and given the operational name Highjump," records Dr. Salla.

"The naval component of Operation Highjump was known as Task Force 68 and comprised 4700 military personnel, one aircraft carrier (the USS Philippine Sea among the largest of all carriers of the time), and a number of naval support ships and aircraft," Dr. Salla adds.

Notably, Admiral Byrd revealed in a press interview that they encountered a new enemy that "could fly from pole to pole at incredible speeds."

"They encountered a mysterious UFO force that attacked the military expedition destroying several ships and a significant number of planes," further documents Dr. Salla.

According to a statement by Grand Admiral Donitz in 1943, and cited in *Nexus Magazine*, "the German submarine fleet is proud of having built for the Führer, in another part of the world, a Shangri-La land, an impregnable fortress."

A Soviet intelligence report cited by Dr. Michael Salla corroborates accounts by military personnel of UFOs that flew close over the U.S. naval flotilla:

"They fired on the UFOs which did retaliate with deadly effects," Dr. Salla elaborates.

Dr. Salla them cites Lieutenant John Sayerson, who gave his own account, also published in *Nexus Magazine*:

> "The thing shot vertically out of the water at tremendous velocity, as though pursued by the devil, and flew between the masts [of the ship] at such a high speed that the radio antenna oscillated back and forth in its turbulence. An aircraft [Martin flying-boat] from the Currituck that took off just a few moments later was struck with an unknown type of ray from the object, and almost instantly crashed into the sea near our vessel.... About ten miles away, the torpedo-boat Maddox burst into flames and began to sink... Having personally witnessed this attack by the object that flew out of the sea, all I can say is, it was frightening." ("Our Real 'War of the Worlds'")

The world that you think you live in is the world that YouTube wants you to live in.

The secretive organizational setting of YouTube yields great power over the visual media of the internet as an extension of this corresponding setting of its Google parent organization. Such a milieu provides the platform for anti-democratic forces to manipulate and undermine democratic society.

Most historians, and people in general, would argue that Nazi Germany lost World War II, but it's apparent that they really didn't.

The COVID-19 pandemic and YouTube's role in it is consistent with the continued presence of a Nazi ego with the alleged support of a "UFO matrix."

Dr. Salla has referred to this prevailing matrix as "MIEC," or the "military-industrial complex of extraterrestrial interests," which he has outlined in detail.

This book contains transcripts of four interviews by learned people banned by YouTube. This silencing of truth betrays a modernized version of the techniques used by the Nazis in their efforts to rise to power.

In a democracy, free speech is valued and supported.

The managers of YouTube, like the leaders of the Nazi movement, lack a fundamental respect for free speech. Nazis viewed free speech to be "harmful" in the same manner that the managers of YouTube deleted the interviews that follow, calling them "harmful," even though the hundreds of comments about these interviews before they were deleted suggests otherwise.

In their rise to power, the Nazis burned many thousands of books. The managers of YouTube "burn" videos for similar reason.

Nazi Germany's elites sought to label scientists and doctors who espoused the prejudices of the Nazi regime as "experts," and everything said by them as truth; any opposing representations were labelled "misinformation." Similarly, YouTube now labels all opposition to the World Health Organization (WHO) and the big businesses making billions of dollars from an experimental COVID-19 "vaccine" as "misinformation." The result is that the WHO is now being used by Google's YouTube clique to strategically enable the construction of a totalitarian society where all critics of the Cabal—and their representatives in the WHO—are to be silenced under the propagandist pretext of public health.

The WHO is the very organization that allowed COVID-19 to escape containment and spread to the rest of the world. And this disaster would have been preventable if not for the disinformation disseminated by the WHO that we should not worry about COVID-19 in China.

Indeed, why create alarm and contain COVID-19 in China before it was able to spread and create fear and panic so that big pharma could have a chance of making billions through jabs?

If the public were empowered to challenge the dubious direction of the WHO from the get-go, there might not have been a "pandemic" in the first place.

YouTube's role has been to project the dubious narrative of the WHO through concealment and deception by promoting those videos that best complement the Cabal's propaganda machine, which is also evident across mainstream media.

Nazi Germany sought to manipulate information and falsify data that could be used to facilitate social control.

It was Nazi Germany, under Joseph Goebbels as propaganda chief, that sought to leverage what became known as the "Big Lie":

"If you tell a lie big enough and keep repeating it, people will eventually come to believe it. The lie can be maintained only for such time as the State can shield the people from the political, economic and/or military consequences of the lie. It thus becomes vitally important for the State to use all of its powers to repress dissent, for the truth is the mortal enemy of the lie, and thus by extension, the truth is the greatest enemy of the State."

Indeed, most people will not believe that the "pandemic" has been constructed around a big lie thanks to YouTube censorship and general manipulation by the mass media.

This lie that encompasses COVID casualties and the thesis of there having been "chaos in every hospital" is no more real than an episode of sensationalist primetime procedural drama.

The doctors, nurses, and others, including the critically acclaimed doctors whose testimony is documented in this book, who have sought to testify to this fact, have been subjected to systematic interview deletions by YouTube.

Can't you hear the YouTube archons saying something to the effect of "There goes another physician telling the truth! Let's also delete that information and call it misinformation!"?

In plain sight, YouTube decreased views of the videos associated with the transcripts that follow because of the crescendo of public support for the interviews of censored Canadian physicians.

For the *Exposed Part I: The persecution of Canadian Physicians by Organized Medicine during the Pandemic* interview (Appendix 1), YouTube froze views at around 290,000. They then decreased views by several thousand before "burning" the video.

Regarding *Exposed Part II,* which for the moment has not been censored, YouTube decreased views from about 90,000 to about 34,000 within a few days.

YouTube bans videos in the name of "misinformation," while it appears to be manipulating data in a manner designed to convey actual misinformation.

YouTube manipulates such data, just as big tech, big pharma, governments, and Cabal overseers manipulate data regarding the alleged pandemic. They then conceal the true intentions of the so-called vaccine as the only antidote that YouTube, under the direction of the Cabal, will be allowed to show through this medium.

No scientist or physician, no matter how strong their credentials are or how sound their data is, shall be allowed to present their findings on YouTube.

The rejection of scientific truth through open debate and analysis in favour of pseudo-science that mirrors the prejudices and ideology of a single institution was at the core of the Nazi system, and it is this system that morphed into the plot to exterminate Jewish people in the name of pseudo-science.

Likewise, COVID-19 and its vaccine as the "only" antidote rests on little more than dogma, and YouTube doesn't want you to hear or see the evidence right before your eyes of the crimes against humanity perpetrated by a Nazi mind that now extends itself well beyond the confines of Nazi Germany.

"They" don't want you to take Vitamins C and D, ivermectin, or any other method of preventing or treating COVID-19 because that would not support the billions in commercial profit raked in by the manufacturers of the "vaccine" and the broader agenda at play.

The Jewish Virtual Library documents Adolf Hitler's description of the Big Lie in *Mein Kampf*:

> "His primary rules were: never allow the public to cool off; never admit a fault or wrong; never concede that there may be some good in your enemy; never leave room for alternatives; never accept blame; concentrate on one enemy at a time and blame him for everything that goes wrong; people will believe a big lie sooner than a little one; and if you repeat it frequently enough people will sooner or later believe it."

It is clear that the management of the "pandemic" is a tactic right out of Hitler's playbook. It dictates that all roads be directed toward the "vaccine," and that neither the manufacturers of the "vaccine" nor the "vaccine" itself are to be blamed or held to account for resulting injuries and deaths

Censorship in dictatorships has never been about "stopping misinformation," and the dictatorial milieu that YouTube represents has shown that it is no exception to the rule.

YouTube's objective is to conceal the truth about the origins and purpose of the COVID-19 pandemic (Appendices 1–5), so that efforts to bring about the destruction of democracy can continue in safety, away from the prying eyes of the "masses."

As a totalitarian society, Nazi Germany lacked structures of accountability and respect for the due process of law. YouTube correspondingly lacks structures of accountability and respect for due process. They banned *Exposed Part I* once, allowed it back up again, and then banned the identical video again permanently after a second appeal, stipulating it "contradicts the WHO."

Any so-called dispute mechanism in YouTube that is regulated by Google as its parent company is a veritable kangaroo court consistent with the style of justice found in the Nazi's rise to power.

There are many people who would argue that a "secret society" is a "conspiracy theory," but YouTube and its Google parent now seem to operate as just such a secret society.

The following excerpts of a speech by President John F. Kennedy to the American Newspaper Publishers Association on 27 April 1961 in the Waldorf-Astoria Hotel, New York City provides context for appreciating the implications of YouTube's strident censorship of scientific and other debate—not only for American democracy, but democracy around the world—as a result of YouTube's dominant global position as a video sharing site:

> *The very word "secrecy" is repugnant in a free and open society; and we are as a people inherently and historically opposed to secret societies, to secret oaths and to secret proceedings.*
>
> *We decided long ago that the dangers of excessive and unwarranted concealment of pertinent facts far outweighed the dangers which are cited to justify it. Even today, there is little value in opposing the threat of a closed society by imitating its arbitrary restrictions. Even today, there is little value in insuring the survival of our nation if our traditions do not survive with it. And there is very grave danger that an announced need for increased security will be seized upon by those anxious to expand its meaning to the very limits of official censorship and concealment.*
>
> *That I do not intend to permit to the extent that it is in my control. And no official of my Administration, whether his rank is high or low, civilian or military, should interpret my words here tonight as an excuse to censor the news, to stifle dissent, to cover up our mistakes or to withhold from the press and the public the facts they deserve to know.*
>
> *For we are opposed around the world by a mono-lithic and ruthless conspiracy that relies primarily on covert means for expanding its sphere of influence — on infiltration instead of invasion, on subversion instead of elections, on intimidation instead of free choice, on guerrillas by night instead of armies by*

day. It is a system which has conscripted vast human and material resources into the building of a tightly knit, highly efficient machine that combines military, diplomatic, intelligence, economic, scientific and political operations.

Its preparations are concealed, not published. Its mistakes are buried, not headlined. Its dissenters are silenced, not praised. No expenditure is questioned, no rumour is printed, no secret is revealed. It conducts the Cold War, in short, with a war-time discipline no democracy would ever hope or wish to match.

No President should fear public scrutiny of his program. For from that scrutiny comes understanding; and from that understanding comes support or opposition.

Without debate, without criticism, no Administration and no country can succeed — and no republic can survive. That is why the Athenian lawmaker Solon decreed it a crime for any citizen to shrink from controversy. And that is why our press was protected by the First Amendment — the only business in America specifically protected by the Constitution — not primarily to amuse and entertain, not to emphasize the trivial and the sentimental, not to simply "give the public what it wants"— but to inform, to arouse, to reflect, to state our dangers and our opportunities, to indicate our crises and our choices, to lead, mould, educate and sometimes even anger public opinion.

Ensuring that all organizations within a society operate within the law helps to protect societies from conspiracy. The only reason to intentionally set up organizations that operate in secrecy and outside of transparent structures of public accountability is to enable them to orchestrate conspiracies free of legal boundaries. Anyone who thinks that conspiracies are not being actively plotted by such organizations against its own citizenry is dreaming in technicolour. They operate in secrecy to enable nefarious conspiratorial actions. Conspiracies in such societies are historically verifiable and are not limited to theory.

The pages that follow contain criticisms that YouTube and its Cabal have sought to deny for your review as a member of a democratic society who values such discussion (Appendices 1–5).

YouTube and the Cabal have an agenda regarding the COVID-19 pandemic, and it is not for your own good. Concealment through censorship is their way of denying your access to critical information that would enable you, along with your communities, to make more informed choices in relation to your health and well being

Thanks to the embracing after World War II of the same "scientists" and "doctors" who perpetrated the Holocaust and the destruction of millions of other lives, we now have psychopaths and sociopaths running this planet. The followers of these psychopaths and sociopaths are using the pandemic as their "coming out party."

This Cabal is tired of running this planet from the shadows. They want to be the official face of the planet, along with the demonic predators that they have sought to serve.

What some people call the Mandela effect is evidence that they are opening up a dimensional portal to the Gates of Hell, which has subjected this planet, the humans, and even animals, to bizarre but surgical changes to the time-line, affecting anything from pop culture to geography, and also notably increasing tendencies for evil and deception among elites.

Only those who have been described as the Mandela affected seem to be noticing these changes, providing context to the Cabal's creation of a realm in which most humans go blindly to get their jabs without questions about what they are really putting into their bodies.

Indeed, these are the kind of questions that have been in the minds of many people in Hassidic Jewish communities who have memories of the Holocaust fresh in their minds about the people who blindly followed the Nazis without question.

YouTube and its Google parent would have us blindly follow the Archons into the Brave New World Order that they seek to expedite through the destruction of free speech and debate, as well as through the repression of scientific data, and the truth along with it.

"We'll know our disinformation program is complete when everything the American public believes is false," said William J. Casey, director of the CIA from 1913-1987, in a statement at his first CIA staff meeting (1981, documents Quote.org.).

If the shadows that run YouTube have their way, no doctors will be allowed to use their knowledge independently to serve the interests of patients based upon the axiom of "do no harm." Instead, in a Brave New World that YouTube is inspiring, doctors will only be allowed to practice medicine if they blindly serve the desires of the shareholders of large pharmaceutical companies to maximize commercial profit, irrespective of medical harm. Such a world that YouTube is pointing us toward is void of integrity and ethics. In this world, science is not a by-product of rigorous analysis and open debate, but instead the result of clandestine committees under the control of archons who decide the truth based upon oppressive and self-serving ideological and commercial objectives.

In his article "Twilight of the Psychopaths," Dr. Kevin Barrett documents 9/11 as being a false flag operation of the Cabal—the very same Cabal that now gives the world its "pandemic":

"It was their terror of losing control that they projected onto the rest of us by blowing up the Twin Towers and inciting temporary psychopathic terror-rage in the American public."

So, why the zealous censorship at YouTube? As Dr. Barrett wrote long before the "pandemic," the Cabal fears losing control because its world is based upon a tissue of lies:

"It is threatened by the spread of knowledge. The greatest fear of any psychopath is of being found out. As George H. W. Bush said to journalist Sarah McClendon in December, 1992, "If the people knew what we had done, they would chase us down the street and lynch us."

In the book entitled *Extraterrestrials Among Us*, by George Andrews, Khyla, a self-represented benevolent alien, is attributed as saying the following:

> "Humanity is not about to be invaded. Humanity is not in the middle of an invasion. Humanity has been invaded! The invasion has taken place, and is nearly in its final stages. Great invasions do not happen with thundering smoke and nuclear weaponry. That is the mark of an immature society. Great invasions happen in secrecy."

Biological warfare is the most efficient way to destroy a population while protecting planetary resources and infrastructure for the alien group that seeks to take over.

Secrecy enables such an alien agenda to continue in a veil of censorship, propaganda, mass manipulation, and gaslighting.

Before humanity can ever expect to reach the land of "milk and honey," we must begin to ask the right kinds of questions about the reality around us. This includes a complete and thorough collective examination of the real origins of COVID-19; the actual ingredients of the jab, as documented in the book *Justin Trudeau and the COVID-19 Biometric Vaccine Totalitarian Agenda*; and other questions that YouTube has sought to oppress in support of deception, manipulation and evil.

Appendix 1

Exposed: The Persecution of Canadian Physicians

Dr. Sam Dubé: THE VIEWS and opinions expressed in this interview are protected by section two of the *Canadian Charter of Rights and Freedoms*, which affirms the freedom of conscience, thought, belief, opinion, and expression, including freedom of the press and other media of communication. If you seek the official narrative on the COVID-19 pandemic, go to the Health Canada website. With that said, if you seek the repressed truth, stay tuned for our interview.

Dr. Sam Dubé: Hello, my name is Dr. Sam Dubé, and I'm a non-clinical physician. I'm also a retired faculty member in university for engineering mathematics, and a strength and conditioning coach with some experience in sports broadcasting. I am here today with four Canadian physicians and their legal representations. Our purpose is to expose the atrocious treatment of these physicians by their medical governing bodies. That is, their provincial medical governing bodies. And to show the public what's actually happening during this, uh, alleged pandemic with, uh, people who have your best interests at heart, that is, uh, your physicians, your physicians themselves.

So I'm here today with Dr. Chris Milburn, Dr. Francis Christian, Dr. Charles Hoffe, and Dr. Roger Hodkinson. They're joined by their legal representation in these persecutions by, uh, John Carpay, Esq. So I want to thank you gentlemen for joining us, and we have a job to do. So Chris, without further ado, could you please introduce yourself?

Dr. Chris Milburn: Sure. So my name is Chris Milburn. I, am a born and bred Cape Bretoner, but the typical story: I had a grandfather who was a coal miner. I actually live on the footprint of the hospital. I was born in Sydney. I had a long journey away from home for 17 years and drifted back after a master's degree in physics, uh, medical degree training and, uh, family and emergency medicine. I have an interest in sports med and injury rehab. Uh, I've done emergency family, but also relevant to this story, I have a fairly intense interest in public health. I was four years on a committee. It's called the CHCP, a committee on healthcare and promotion, which dealt with issues of broader healthcare, public health at Canadian Medical Association. For my last year, I was the chair of that committee, and I believe it's been about six or seven years on the Doctors Nova Scotia public health committee, and just finished my two year tenure as a head of that committee. It doesn't get into, I've been on numerous local community health boards. So I have a long interest in public health, and it's given me a certain perspective on COVID planning.

Dr. Sam Dubé: Wonderful. Thank you, Chris. Charles, could you please introduce yourself to our viewers?

Dr. Charles Hoffe: Yes. Uh, my name is Charles Hoffe. I'm a family physician and emergency room physician. I did my medical training in South Africa. I came to Canada in 1990, so I've been, in Canada. I've been a dyed in the wool, rural GP and emergency physician for 31 years, and so the last 28 of those have been in Lytton, British Columbia.

Dr. Sam Dubé: Wonderful. Thank you, Charles. Francis, would you tell our viewers exactly who you are, please?

Dr. Francis Christian: Thanks, Sam. Uh, my name is Francis Christian. Uh, I've been a surgeon for more than 20 years. Um, I have a fellowship, uh, from the Royal College of surgeons of Edinburgh, and I have a fellowship from the Royal College of Surgeons of Canada. Um, up until the 23rd of June, I was the director of, uh, quality improvement and patient safety in the department of surgery in the University of Saskatchewan. Um, my designation was also clinical professor. I was also the director of a surgical humanities program. I had actually started the department of QI and patient safety several years ago.

Um, and amongst multiple other activities I had started for the department, the NSQUIP program was a national surgical quality improvement program. Um, I also founded the Surgical Quality and Safety Committee, the SQSC, which I co-chaired with the department head, and, uh, together with our university's computer department. I developed an app, uh, it's called the M&M app, which is still available on, uh, the Google Play Store and the App Store for Apple, uh, devices. And interestingly, the M&M app is now being used across the province of Saskatchewan. Uh, I co-founded the surgical humanities program for the department, and I'm the editor of the Journal of the Surgical Humanities, which I founded, uh. The fall of 2020 issue of the journal had much in it about the COVID-19 pandemic, actually, including my editorial. And if you go to the department of surgery website, they still have the PDF archive of issues right up to the fall of 2020 issue.

Dr. Sam Dubé: Wonderful. Thank you, Francis. And Roger, could you please give us your background?

Dr. Roger Hodkinson: Sure. Yeah, very briefly. A Cambridge graduate, came to Canada in 1970 when it was a very different place. I'm sure we'll talk about that. Um, been an assistant professor at the university; had done loads of teaching over the years. Um, the president of our provincial association of pathologists, um, done a lot of world college work, chairman of the examination committee in general pathology. Um, I'm currently the, uh, the CEO of a biotech company in North Carolina. Um, I practiced in the States, I practice in Britain, general practice in Canada and the states. Um, but my biggest credential is none of the above. Um, my biggest credential is I was the only chairman of action on smoking and health for many years, where I learnt, um, the smarts, you might say, of how to take on government, um, as, uh, taking on big tobacco, the predatory marketing practices, probably saved more lives in that role than I ever did as a pathologist. And, um, I'm very proud of it.

Dr. Sam Dubé: Thank you so much, Roger. And finally, John.

Dr. John Carpay: I'm John Carpay, I'm a lawyer. I was born in the Netherlands. I came to Canada at the age of seven and grew up in British Columbia. I earned a political science degree at, uh, Université Laval in Quebec and, uh, thereafter did a law degree at the University of Calgary, and I've been working in, uh, public interest law, uh, defending charter rights and freedoms on a full-time basis since, uh, 2005. And, uh, I head up the Justice Centre for Constitutional Freedoms. We are a public interest law firm. We have clients all over the country. We've got uh, about a dozen lawyers on staff and looking to hire more in these very dark times. Uh, we wanna, we need some more lawyers and, uh, I feel very honored and privileged to represent courageous people, uh, all of our clients without exception, uh, including the doctors here today, but all of the people are, uh, displaying, tremendous courage in standing up to government tyranny and government violation of rights and freedoms. So that's me.

Dr. Sam Dubé: Thank you so much, John. It's wonderful to have you here today in your, uh, your support, personal and professional. Um, just to contextualize, it is Canada Day today. So happy Canada Day everyone. And I think it is strangely appropriate because we have representation of our physicians. Um, Chris is, uh, broadcasting from Moncton, I believe. And, uh, Francis, you are coming to us from Saskatchewan. Am I correct?

Dr. Francis Christian: Saskatoon, Saskatchewan.

Dr. Sam Dubé: Saskatchewan and, uh, Charles. Now Charles has an interesting situation because he just evacuated from Lytton British Columbia last night, and his office has been burnt, um, to a crisp unfortunately. So, um, he actually called me on a mountain road on the way to Kamloops, to be with his family. So Charles, our hearts go out to you. And so sorry about that. And, uh, hopefully Lytton can recover from that. So, you know, we're doubly thankful for you being here with us today and, of course, Roger is in Edmonton. So we have multiple provinces represented spanning Canada. John, where are you exactly, again?

John Carpay, Esq.: I'm in Calgary.

Dr. Sam Dubé: You're in Calgary as well, okay. And I'm in Ottawa right now. So now I guess we had to mention the Capital somewhere there. So there certainly is an appropriateness to this in addressing this issue. So what I'd like to do is I would like to leave it to each physician to talk to us as to why they're here, what their story is, and how they ended up getting persecuted by the very governing body that was supposedly out to protect people, their patients. And that really the only thing that, uh, these physicians here, ladies and gentlemen are guilty of is trying to protect you and expressing a discontent and a concern with the, uh, official narrative and the public health response to this pandemic. So without further ado, um, I would like to ask Dr. Chris Milburn to please tell us your story.

Dr. Chris Milburn: Well, my story actually predates COVID. Um, I was, I first, um, had a head-on with cancel culture back in late 2019 when I wrote an editorial piece for the *Chronicle Herald*, which is our biggest newspaper in, um, in Nova Scotia. And my editorial was just about, uh, the difficulty of dealing with violent patients in custody and how that was very fraught for physicians and other staff who had to deal with these patients and where was the balance of individual rights and individual responsibility and all that. And my piece was overall very well received except by what you probably call the left-wing fringe. And for my troubles, I got a complaint signed by a number of, um, complainants who were, whose names were kept anonymous, JCCF, thank you, John, uh, helped me through the complaint process and we eventually lobbied the college to make it public, but the basis of the complaint was that I used such words as criminal, which was stigmatizing to patients. And I clearly wasn't compassionate enough to be a doctor, et cetera, et cetera. So was it a difficult time for me?

And I went through that during COVID and in a time where I was bound to secrecy. So I couldn't actually seek support, uh, during COVID as I mentioned, I have a strong interest in public health. I'm pretty good with numbers. You know, I have graduate level math and, um, I began, I started independent, like I think many of us, we saw what was happening in Bergamo, Italy and then New York City. And we thought, oh my God, what is this? Uh, is it the bubonic plague? And I was all for a precautionary approach when we started, but I think the, uh, the difference for me was that quite quickly I saw that the numbers were not what they originally seemed in that this was not the killer of all ages that we had to be really concerned about.

Um, and so I started to change my tune. I just, I tried my best to follow the science, but it seemed like the more I followed the science, the more that put me at odds with our, uh, prevailing orthodoxy. Um, it was pretty chilling for us, when it reached here in Nova Scotia, in March, our... our college put out this following statement, they emailed it to all physicians:

> *Physicians continue to meet their professional obligations of complying with public health COVID-19 guidance. As well, physicians on the front lines are providing important education to their patients regarding public health, safety, and vaccination information.*

This all sounds sort of benign, but then they get into ...

> *...[T]he vast majority of the profession is modelling, compliance, and as such there has been a little problem with anti-maskers or anti-vaxxers.*

So I certainly don't like that statement because it suggests that someone like me, who thinks that maybe the mask rules are a little bit draconian or that patients should have autonomy in choosing vaccine. I could be considered either an anti-masker or an anti-vaxxer because those statements aren't scientific in nature. They're not well-defined.

But most chilling -

> ...[T]he college wishes to recognize the leadership that physicians are playing in supporting this unanimity so key to our success in combating COVID...

And, that's where, to me, it went completely off the rails. Um, I don't know about the other folks, but when I read my Hippocratic Oath, there was nothing about unanimity in it. And, uh, I never agreed to be unanimous with all my colleagues. They never agreed to be unanimous with me. As a matter of fact, I thought it was quite healthy and necessary for scientific progress for us to disagree often and vigorously, and to work those disagreements out and to figure out what's best for our patients.

So I am quite sure... with this recent, I spoke out against certain things, against mandatory vaccinations, and I spoke out against school closures on a radio program. For my troubles I was removed as my job as the head of ER for our zone. And I'm quite sure at this point, there's a Twitter mob that had been organizing as of a few weeks ago to organize everyone, to send complaints to the college. So I'm quite sure I'm going to be dealing with more college complaints over my stance.

So, um, I'm butting up for the second time in two years against cancel culture for speaking my mind. And I just, you know, as the other folks I'm sure will agree. I just think that's extremely unhealthy for science, that it was somebody who disagreed that the Earth was flat, that proved it was round. It was somebody who disagreed that the Earth was the centre of the universe and prove that it wasn't. And we need to allow dissenters. Most of us won't be bright by the nature of this. Most of us will be off the rails and proven wrong, that's fine, but that's science and we're shutting that down at this point.

Dr. Sam Dubé: Well, you know, consensus, as I mentioned to Charles last night was four out of five physicians prefer camels [a brand of cigarettes], right? So, I mean, some of us are old enough to remember that and Thalidomide. And what else out there, what else out there? I mean the number of examples is almost endless. So Chris, how did this affect you personally? Um, and you alluded to some professionally here, if you can just elaborate on that a little bit for us, give our viewers some insight.

Dr. Chris Milburn: Sure. So I'm, you know, I'm a very kind of geeky guy. I read a lot, in my spare time. I ride my bike. I have cats, I have a great wife, but I also really really liked my job. And I like looking after patients and what happened to me last year in the midst of the complaint. Um, it took a lot of my time away from patient care. The time that I could have spent taking care of patients in a province that's really, really understaffed for doctors instead of spending days and days and days working on letters and talking with lawyers from JCCF and some sleepless nights about my future, is this the right profession for me? If I can't have free speech, should I be a doctor? So it was a very, a very hard time for me that took me away from the things that I really like to do. And it was very stressful. Uh, I'm an old hat at it now. So this time around, it's probably not quite as bad, and I've learned not to take things very personally.

Um, so, you know, it's interesting. And then probably, you know, all the other doctors on this call will be having the same experience that, on the one hand I have kind of what I'd say, the left-wing fringe Twitter mob, who want my head on a pike, or run me out of town with pitchforks at minimum. But on the other hand, I've been contacted by hundreds and hundreds of people from across the country. Just saying, thank you for speaking out. Even people who actually said, I don't agree with you, but thank you for speaking out, because I think we need to have a discussion about these things. And I think that's important. So I guess at times like this, it shows you who your true friends are and who you can really have a real conversation and a meaningful discussion with them. I'm learning that bit by bit by bit.

Dr. Sam Dubé: That's wonderful for sharing that with us. Chris, thank you so much. And I'm going to ask John Carpay, who is your legal representation to comment on your cases and, uh, give us, uh, you know, kind of a legal overview and to any insights that he might have, and, uh, you know, talk about this response that you received and, uh, and look at it, uh, from a bigger picture. John, can you please address this?

Dr. John Carpay: The Colleges of Surgeons and Physicians, the colleges are government bodies and the supreme law of the land is the *Canadian Charter of Rights and Freedoms*, not any public health order, and the colleges are actually required to comply with the Charter because they are a government body. So one of the things that colleges must do is respect freedom of speech and in various Supreme Court of Canada decisions, uh, the rationale for free speech includes, uh, the search for truth and public discourse and finding, uh, determination of good laws, which really cannot take place if there's one orthodoxy. There's no debate, uh, about laws and what the law ought to be. Um, so there's, free speech was one of the, uh, pillars of the free society. Uh, in fact, it's been said that if you lost all of your rights and freedoms, but retained your freedom of speech, you could use your freedom of speech to gain all the other ones back. But if you lose your freedom of speech, you're no longer even in a position to defend your religious freedom, your freedom of association, your freedom of conscience, your freedom not to be locked up in a prison hotel, uh, upon returning to Canada, et cetera, et cetera, et cetera. If there's no freedom of speech, uh, the whole free society, crumbles, democracy crumbles.

Now there is a place for colleges to, uh, uphold standards, standards of behaviour, standards of, uh, professional conduct. You know, doctors should not have sexual relations with a patient. A doctor has to, uh, ensure a patient has informed consent. So there's a whole code of ethics, and there's nothing wrong with having a formal body that, uh, promotes and enforces a code of ethics. Um, and there could even be a place for the college to make some determinations about medical practices. I'm aware that the Ontario college, for example, has, uh, banned, uh, female genital mutilation, uh, also known as female circumcision and a physician may not perform that service. May not refer for that service... So there can be, there can be a time and a place for the college to step in, uh, and, uh, uh, maybe shut down debate on an extreme example like that. Uh, but to squelch, uh, debate on very unsettled matters, uh, lockdowns are a brand new experiment.

Uh, I've asked numerous, uh, pro lockdown people. Can you cite me one example in human history of any society, any country, any civilization that has succeeded in vanquishing a virus by destroying its economy and by shredding the fabric of civil society? And so, you know, the answer is none. So this is an experiment and it's not scientific to insist on the correctness of the experiment and, uh, silence debate about the experiment. So I'll pause there and have more comments later on.

Dr. Sam Dubé: Yeah, absolutely. Because when we get to, uh, the physicians cases here, and I mean, not even giving reasons why they're making statements against these, uh, the physicians who are, uh, expressing their concern and questioning, not even giving any reasons, you know, so thank you for that, John. Um, I'd like to move on to, uh, Dr. Charles Hoffe. So Charles, can you tell us what happened to you?

Dr. Charles Hoffe: Yes. Uh, so my story of persecution by the medical authorities all began, um, in about mid-March, um, when the vaccine rollout was in about its third month and there was significant evidence of harm. And at that point, 12 countries in Europe had shut down the, um, AstraZeneca vaccine because of serious evidence of life-threatening clots. And so my problems all began because I sent an email to a group of coworkers, and they were doctors, nurses, and pharmacists in our area who were literally involved in this vaccine rollout. And, basically, I expressed my ethical concerns with continuing to roll out a vaccine that had clear evidence of harm. And, basically, I mean, I was aware that this was, this new gene-based vaccine idea had never been tried on human beings before this pandemic. And there had been no animal trials, which are normally mandatory for any new vaccine.

And there was no long-term safety data. So this was clearly an experiment. And there's a foundational ethical principle in clinical trials when you're trying out a new experimental therapy, that you need to be monitoring your subjects carefully. And if there's any evidence of harm, you stop the experiment; it's on purely ethical grounds. And so I basically sent this email saying, there's clear evidence of harm. Do you think we should be paus-ing this? It was literally just a question. Do you think we should be pausing this to take stock? So within 48 hours, I received quite a reprimand from the local medical authorities to tell me that I was seriously out-of-line and that I was guilty of causing "vaccine hesitancy." And so, um, and this was seen as a patient safety issue, and I said to them, but hang on, giving an experimental vaccine that is clearly causing harm is also a patient safety issue.

I mean that is my motivation, is patient safety, but obviously we were looking at this from different ends, where their whole purpose was just vaccinate everybody. And my purpose was hang on if it's harming people, this is not the solution. And so I was told that I was *not allowed to say anything negative about this vaccine* in our emergency department, where I work as an emergency doctor. And I was told that if I had any questions about this, that I was not to address them to my colleagues, but to the medical health officer for our region in charge of the vaccine rollout. And that my vaccine, my "crime of vaccine hesitancy" would be reported to the College of Physicians and Surgeons of BC. So I accepted this, I said, okay I won't say anything. And I will send my concerns to the MHO.

So, I had actually been, this was now 9 or 10 weeks since these people... since my patients had got their vaccine, but I'd been away, I'd been in away in South Africa. And I just arrived back. So just my first week back at work. And then in the days that followed patients started coming into my office that had very clear evidence of harm. And in other words, it wasn't just reports from Europe or from elsewhere. It was my own patients. So at this point, I got even more concerned about patient safety because I could see the problems firsthand. This wasn't just other people's reports. These were my patients. And so I sent a letter to our MHO as they had asked, and I expressed all my concerns and got no answers. So then I drafted a letter to our, um, our provincial health officer, Dr. Bonnie Henry. And because I was told she doesn't reply to letters, colleagues that said, you know, there's no point in just sending her a letter, it's going to go nowhere. You need to send it as an open letter. So I sent it as an open letter and basically it was all around what my whole motivation is, patient safety and medical ethics. And so I said to her, basically there's clear evidence of harm in my patients; what is the mechanism of entry?

This is a medically induced disease. What is it, what's happening and how should I as their doctor be treating this? And of course I didn't expect, but that was my question. And then I also put the question, you know, whenever an experimental treatment is being tried and there's clear evidence of harm, we're supposed to shut her down. *Shouldn't we be doing that?* So this was a huge problem. So that letter has continued to go around the world. And I get emails from Hong Kong and New Zealand and Europe, and continuously day by day people reading that letter, which I sent in the beginning of April, that's three months ago. So, anyway, I sent that letter off and it caused a bit of a stir, but our local health authority who had told me I wasn't allowed to say anything bad about this was clearly very upset for me causing even more "vaccine hesitancy."

And so they were determined to find something to shut me down on. So they were looking very closely. And so after about two or three weeks, I got a phone call followed by an email telling me that my clinical privileges to work as an emergency physician were being instantly suspended on two grounds. Um, firstly, that I had encouraged a nurse to tell people to refuse the vaccine. And the second was that I had posted misinformation about COVID and, interestingly enough, so I'll tell you what these were, because it is just absolutely absurd. They were clearly desperate to find something to accuse me of. So, I had explained to one of our emergency room nurses, that someone who has had a natural COVID infection does not need the vaccine because they're already immune to COVID. And in fact, there's very good evidence that natural immunity from natural infection is a robust and broad immunity that lasts a long time and is far superior from anything that you can get from a syringe.

Uh, and so by explaining that to a nurse, and actually it was for a patient who had COVID and literally her early symptom from the COVID was losing her appetite for 10 days, that was literally her only symptom. And then she had the vaccine and was quite significantly ill from it. And so she thought something must be desperately wrong because why was the vaccine making her more sick than COVID? So she came in. So I said to the nurse, and this was on the telephone, please just tell her she doesn't need the second dose. And I explained to the nurse, the whole scientific rationale about she doesn't need a vaccination against something that she's already immune to. And on the basis of that, I was accused of encouraging nurses to tell patients to refuse the vaccine. And the misinformation that I was accused of was that I was accused of posting a printout from the JCCF of COVID mortality statistics, according to age categories on the notice board, which they decided was misleading because it basically showed that two thirds of all the people that have died of COVID in BC are over the age of 70.

And they didn't like people to know that because they want children vaccinated as well. And so this was seen as being "misinformation." So on the basis of those two things, they suspended my clinical privileges to work as an emergency physician. So for me, the personal and professional cost of that was because I do both jobs. I'm an emergency physician and a family physician, and I do them simultaneously. Actually, in a small town… you're looking for the same people in the ER, as you are in the office… one is just an urgent problem and the other isn't. So I basically lost 50% of my income, uh, immediately, was the effect of that…but it also means that because I now have this black mark against me in my professional record, if I decided to work somewhere else, I wouldn't be allowed to do that because I now have this charge against me, um, and the suspension. So it significantly hampers all future employment opportunities for me. Um, and so that's, but the motive, my primary motivation is patient safety and medical ethics. And so that's my story on that was the cost to me.

Dr. Sam Dubé: Hasn't it been said about physicians, I mean, our adages are do no harm and informed consent. You know, we need to talk about this more, you know.

Dr. Charles Hoffe: That is the foundation of why we do what we do. I mean, informed consent is mandatory by law. And there's no informed consent with the COVID shots because people are not being told what the risks are at all. Um, and they're not being told what the benefits are at all. I mean, most people think they're going to be immune to COVID and then get told they still need to wear a mask, you know, which is obviously they're not, otherwise they wouldn't still have to wear a mask. Effectively, the antibodies are in the wrong place. Do you know the antibodies you get from the vaccine are in your blood, but you get COVID through your respiratory tract. And those two, uh, those two systems of immunity are independent of one another. And you can only be, you'll only get immunity to COVID through natural infection, because then you will have antibodies in your respiratory tract.

Dr. Sam Dubé: You know, and this is what we're all taught in medical school. Right? And this whole idea of natural immunity trumping vaccine immunity, it's almost a no brainer for us. And yet they're systematically removing references to natural immunity. It's now become a footnote. They mentioned it occasionally. And I'll talk about that a little bit later, but just before we, uh, digress with the, uh, the medical aspect. John could you please comment as to, uh, um, comment on Charles' case here, please, and how the college responded.

John Carpay, Esq.: I'm very sorry to learn of these details. Um, maybe it's surprising to hear me say, you know, learn of them. I've got, there's 12 lawyers on staff that are intimately familiar, so generally familiar with, uh, Charles's story, but I'm deeply grieved. There's a bunch of new details here that, uh, I wasn't aware of and, you know, getting back to the free speech and free society angle.... um it's one of the core characteristics of totalitarianism is this putting forward, you know... The government decides what the truth is, and then enforces that. And there's no more debate about what is truth. What is fact, it's all about promoting this, uh, this ideology. So we have an ideology that, uh, in various columns that I've written, I've called it COVIDism or lockdownism, and it's just the ideology that lockdowns are, uh, not only the best solution, but the only solution and everything else is off the table.

Uh, you know, whether vitamin D uh, is a good preventative or a good aid, uh, or ivermectin or anything else, uh, that's off the table, uh, whether we would have achieved the same results without lockdowns based on voluntary changes in people's behaviour. Um, and even the death stats, you know, I'm very grateful for the fact that in Alberta and other provinces, the government does list the stats, the information on the justice centre website, uh, we all get, we use government statistics. We don't go to some conspiracy websites, but, you know, Alberta health services, uh, tells us that, uh, on its website, that three quarters of the people dying with COVID are elderly and have three or more serious health conditions, uh, cancer, emphysema, heart disease, et cetera. 75% of the deaths involve people with three or more serious conditions. This is a relevant fact, and yet, uh, a totalitarian government will shut things down, but of course they need a pretext. They need a justification. So they say misinformation, and that's just a very convenient way to, uh, to shut down speech.

Dr. Sam Dubé: Thank you. Thank you, John. I'd like to move on to Francis. Francis your story is I think among our most recent and, uh, I have to admit, uh, when I heard, uh, the recording that we're going to allude to, and that will be to the end of this video for our viewers to listen to, uh, my stomach turned, my stomach turned at what you had to endure. It was so Orwellian. It was gaslighting. And I'm so sorry you had to go through that. I just have to say that. Okay. Like, honestly, I don't know how you dealt with that, but, um, could you please tell us what happened?

Dr. Francis Christian: Uh, thank you, Sam. Um, so what happened, uh, was on the 23rd of June, uh, just over a week ago, uh, I was called into what was termed a WebEx meeting with the Dean of the medical college here, the chief medical officer, and the interim head of the Department. I was stripped of my university faculty position and fired from my roles as Director of QI quality improvement and patient safety and fired from my role as the Director of Surgical Humanities program. Now, my offence or "crime" was supposedly asking for informed consent from parents and children in the rollout of the Pfizer COVID-19 vaccine to our children and Saskatchewan. Um, you know, many of us in the medical profession have a similar journey, uh, to what Chris was alluding to initially. And I›m talking about March of last year. I did believe some of the official narratives. At least I thought this is a new virus. We need some time to take stock to see what›s happening. And, uh, I was a little bit sceptical about the way lockdowns were implemented. And then in May I started asking questions. You know why, Sam. It›s because they were for the first time ever that I can remember in my professional career, major world-class scientific voices were being censored, were being suppressed. Um, to give you an example, uh, there were some very early voices that argued against lockdowns and they came out with what is called a Great Barrington Declaration. It included, um, people of great eminence, uh, Martin Kulldorff, who has since become a friend, but not only does Kulldorff hold a professorship in Harvard, he is an epidemiologist whose software is actually being used on the field in epidemiology, uh, programs around the world.

He's a leader in his field. He is, um, he's somebody who, before this COVID thing started, was, uh, you know, the fellow who set vaccine policy together with some other experts. And then it had Sutra Gupta from Oxford and a fellow called Jay Bhattacharya from Stanford and they were censoring them. And the pattern of the censorship was very interesting, uh, for those of us who have studied Soviet history, which I have, and I've studied the Nazi system a little less, but, uh, the Soviets were very good in weaponizing words. So misinformation, dis-information, and the media started using those words. And then they would always follow with not what the Soviet commissars said, but what *experts* say. And they would never define who these experts were or how they matched the experts on the other side. They were always inferior to these world-leading voices, but they were given prominence and everything that the experts said was misinformation or disinformation.

So I started asking questions, uh, and becoming sceptical of the official narratives. I was, uh, trying to influence the system from within here in Saskatoon. And then, um, they started, uh, earlier this year, rolling out the vaccines at literally warp speed to our kids without parental, um, and, children having informed consent and informed consent is not a controversial topic at all. It's something that the profession has held dear, has held as a basic tenant in medicine for hundreds of years. What it means very simply is you tell the patient or the person, what are the risks of the intervention. What are the benefits? And are there any alternatives? And, uh, I gave a press conference, which miraculously was covered by the mainstream press here.

Um, and, uh, essentially asked the government to pause the whole program because children and parents were not being given informed consent. Uh, and I read in my statement exactly what informed consent should look like at a very basic level. For example, this is an experimental technology. It hasn't been tried in humans before, uh. How many parents know that and how many children know that? Shouldn't children and parents know that? And then that this vaccine has only interim authorization in Canada and what is called emergency use authorization in the United States. And, um, and I pointed out that full authorization takes several years and includes multiple safety considerations. Uh, I pointed out the fact that, uh, in the VAER system, the vaccine adverse events reporting system, uh, in the United States, uh, there were, at that time more than 6,000 deaths, I pointed out this, uh, this is an association and not a causation, but it's a strong signal and it cannot be ignored.

And, um, and then I said that this particular vaccine for kids is already showing harm. It's showing a condition called myocarditis. And, uh, as we were discussing this various bodies around the world, the, Swedish, uh, vaccine agency, the German agency had already said that the German vaccine agency had made very clear recommendations that it, you know, only very, uh, otherwise sick somebody with leukemia or somebody, a kid with immunocompromised should be vaccinated with this vaccine. And otherwise it should be not given to kids. The UK vaccine agency was poised to make a recommendation like that. And, uh I thought that's very basic too, and then I pointed out that for a kid, this is not an emergency. Uh, the risk of dying of COVID is less than the risk of dying of the annual flu; it's 0.003%.

It's been, uh, shown statistically that's really, uh, is statistically zero immeasurable risk. You really can't, in statistics it's very difficult to measure that kind of risk. So for a disease that does not pose a threat to kids, they are using an emergency use authorization vaccine, which hasn't been tested, which is already showing problems. And all this is not really being, uh, being disclosed to both parents and the kids. And, um, I basically read out, uh, very few basic things. And I said, the province is not, uh, achieving this very basic requirement in medicine, which is the taking of informed consent from parents and the kids. And, um, on the 23rd of June, uh, I was called into this WebEx meeting. And, uh, I was fired of all these positions. I was stripped of my university faculty position. My, uh, offence crime was supposedly asking for informed consent from parents and children, um, in the rollout of the Pfizer COVID 19 vaccine.

Um, so, you know, it's very interesting because the local press, the so-called mainstream media who have now become arms of government, by the way that happened in the Soviet Union, too. Um, I don't know whether Canadians know, even the recent history adequately, to realize the creeping totalitarianism that is coming upon us. So in the Soviet Union arms of the media were co-opted to serve the purposes of the communist regime. Same thing happened in Nazi Germany, and, uh, the compliant local mainstream media. They covered my story with largely negative attempted hit pieces, uh, you know, CTV and, uh, the local Post Media newspaper. Uh, I must say Global News was the exception. They carried a fast story, uh, about me, I was on evening news and so on. Uh, and then this tribunal who spoke to me believed it would all end there and they were basking in some sort of a borrowed limelight.

But they were wrong. Uh, first of all, uh, and, uh, John Carpay, uh, and the JCCF deserve all the credit for this, because they saw in this, as I did, something much bigger than the terrible dystopian, um, treatment that I had received at the hands of this tribunal. Uh, and they saw as I did that this was, uh, a, a fundamental assault on everything we took for granted: free speech, the free debate of scientific ideas, and the very, uh, the very thing that has made humanity's existence on earth so much better. And that is a scientific method. All this was under assault, uh, but with friends and supporters, and well-wishes all over the world, including very good doctor friends, you know, Patrick Phillips... my story has been carried all over the world, uh, in major media, in zero hedge and off guardian and alternate media in Twitter in telegram feeds and Facebook.

And I've been getting messages of support from Canada, of course, from across the USA, as far as a field, as Australia, the Netherlands, the UK, uh, JCCF, the Justice Centre for Constitutional Freedoms, Twitter feed had, uh, something like more than 3000 retweets within a few days and all over the world. And this is sad for me because, uh, you know, I don't want, uh, the University of Saskatchewan as deemed the Saskatchewan health authority to get all this negative attention, but the eyes of the world are turned in a very negative manner to Saskatchewan, to the University, to Canada unfortunately. And this is, you know, the state we are in. Uh, hundreds of other internet sites are broadcasting this totalitarian control and dystopia, and very valued friends, colleagues from academia have written letters of support from me to the president of the university, to the Dean, to the CML, to the Deputy Minister of Health.

And, I got to tell you, any of these authorities contemplating action against world-class academics, Byram Bridle, for example, uh, um, anybody contemplating so-called disciplinary dystopian action. Uh, let me put out a warning there. Okay. You may be able to get away with it in the short term, and you may think the mainstream media is going to report very, very well on this dystopian tyranny, but there will be another very notorious publicity that will elevate you. And within, uh, a few hours, your totalitarian tyranny will definitely be known. It'll be known around the world, independent of the mainstream media.

Dr. Sam Dubé: I really hope so, Francis. Thank you so much for your words. Um, you, uh, it's very moving what you went through when you, uh, you summarized a lot of what I think, uh, many of us wanted to say, so thank you for that. John, could you please comment on, uh, on Francis' case and you did hear the audio, uh, of that, uh, meeting the tribunal.

John Carpay, Esq.: The audio, which I believe is going to be added onto the end of this, it's just appalling. Uh, they, they called it a meeting, uh, but it wasn't a meeting. It was more just, we're going to read you this letter, telling you that you are fired and terminated from, uh, from several different positions. And there was no dialogue at all. Uh, I admire for how Francis kept his cool. I wouldn't have come close to, uh, being on that level, uh, at all. And, uh, so that, that was very dystopian, you know, it's interesting. So, uh, Francis and I believe one of the other physicians mentioned that, you know, when lockdowns are first brought down, it seemed like a good idea. And the justice center had the same slow evolution of thought. Uh, it can be quite justified and appropriate under the *Canadian Charter of Rights and Freedoms* for a government to impose temporary measures in the face of either a real crisis or, or a perceived crisis where you have reason to believe that this may be and I remember Dr. Neil Ferguson of Imperial College in London actually compared COVID to the Spanish Flu of 1918. He did.

And of course, as, uh, as many of the viewers will know, that killed between 20 and 50 million people around the world. Some historians say a hundred million at a time when the world population was only a quarter of what it is today. So if COVID was as, deadly as the Spanish Flu of 1918, we would not be looking at a 80 to a hundred to 200 million deaths. And, uh, we're at, you know, three or 4 million. So we have something that's in line with perhaps the, uh, the Asian flu of 1957, uh, the Hong Kong flu of 1968. Those are very bad flus that killed a million or 2 million people when the world's population was less than half of what it is today. Uh, so that's what COVID arguably is in line with. But, uh, we were put into a state of fear, uh, with this prediction. If we had gone, if the Justice Centre had tried to go to court, uh, in March of 2020, there's a hundred percent chance we would've lost because the court would have said, look, we don't know how deadly this is. It could be very deadly. Therefore, all of these restrictions on our rights and freedoms are justified, but for myself in April, I started asking tough questions a month later.

I wrote to all the health ministers and said, can you tell me about the, uh, uh, lockdown consequences, in terms of canceled surgeries, canceled diagnoses, suicide rates, alcoholism, uh, domestic abuse, uh, mental health issues resulting from loneliness and isolation, et cetera, et cetera, et cetera, et cetera. And the worst thing. One of the worst things in the whole situation is that there's not a single government in Canada that has done a proper and thorough costs benefits analysis of the lockdowns. I support free speech for pro lockdown people. If somebody wants to argue that these are good measures and they're scientific and they're saving lives, bring on the debate, but it is utterly irresponsible for governments not to, uh, conduct a proper cost benefit analysis. And that involves necessarily to make a deliberate effort to, uh, to monitor and analyze and explore all the different lockdowns harms.

And they're not doing that. Uh, I'll comment briefly on the media. It has turned into an arm of government. Uh, this is very likely influenced by the fact that the mainstream media or the so-called legacy media are government funded. They get substantial government funding, and we had, uh, the court action that is the most advanced in terms of going through the whole litigation procedure. Uh, we had eight days of trial in Manitoba in the month of May. And at one point, uh, Dr. Jared Bullard, who is an expert witness for the Manitoba government in charge of the Winnipeg labs, admitted in court under oath that 56% of the so-called, uh, positive results, positive on the PCR test, 56% of those people do not have COVID. And do you think the media reported on this, you know, even if you were pro lockdown, but if you were committed to truth and to telling the truth to the public, you would report on the fact that a, uh, government witness in court admitted that 56%, and there's reason to believe it could be much higher, but that's secondary.

The government official admitted that 56% of the PCR test results are, uh, false positives. And these people, 56% at least, do not have COVID. So when the government was engaging in the daily fear-mongering and saying, well, we have another 2000 cases in the past week. Well, at least 56% minimum of those cases are people that the government knows do not have COVID. So fortunately we do have other avenues of, uh, of getting the word out, uh, the justice center. I now take it for granted that our news releases get boycotted by mainstream media. I'm no longer bothered by it, but it gets out on Twitter and Facebook and by way of our website, and we have the Rebel Media, we have True North, we have all kinds of independent media that are getting the word out.

Dr. Sam Dubé: Well, this is really important because, uh, you know, I interviewed Ivory Hecker, who was the young reporter, uh, based in Houston who blew the whistle on Fox News suppressing stories on hydroxychloroquine. In fact, took her off a story and gave her an alternate one. And she had been biding her time for months recording her bosses and such at Fox and finding out where the money was coming from and such. And, uh, interestingly enough, I've been in touch with her since our interview. And she said, so many reporters have come to her and told their stories of how they've been and are continuing to be suppressed in their quest for the truth, having to do with the supposed pandemic and the vaccines and the, I mean, the list goes on and on and on, we can specify. So, um, it's very, very interesting how this is happening in the States, but I think here in Canada, we really need a shot in the arm.

We really need a shot in the arm because our culture's a little different. We tend to be a bit more accepting. We tend to be a bit more trusting with authority. Um, Roger might even say, we just need to wake up, you know, but really we do, we really do, and I love being Canadian. And on this day here in Canada Day, I think it's appropriate that we have physicians and a lawyer from across this great country of ours fighting for what makes Canada, Canada. Right? And Francis put it so aptly, and it's been referred to you know as this totalitarian tic tock. I mean, God, what other term is there to describe this, look at what's happening. That's the bigger picture that Francis was so determined to talk about today. And really this is the beginning of something very, very insidious, very bad.

And it snuck up on us during a time of alleged crisis, you know, and this is what we're dealing with. I'm sorry, I'm rambling on here because I really want Roger to talk to this. And Roger and I have become friends. Um, I interviewed him twice. He, uh, he gave some very wonderful information and as an esteemed and renowned pathologist, um, he comes from another side, you know, you guys all have your specialties. Um, and I actually want to address something that Charles told me last night as well. Uh, when we go into a round table discussion, but, you know, I've had some wonderful chats with Roger. And I would like to hand off to him now and tell us his story and his perspective what's going on. Having heard everything everyone else said. So Roger, please, would you take it away for us?

Dr. Roger Hodkinson: Thank you, Sam. Um, a lot of, um, my feelings have already been expressed and, uh, I'll use the bulk of my time to give you a view as more of an overview you might say of what's going on, um, with the colleges, and the consequences.

Um, but so far as me personally, um, uh, I'm practicing what you might call administrative medicine in companies, and I'm not seeing patients. Um, so I'm rather privileged in that respect, uh, given the ultimate threats of removing my license, because I don't actually need it to do what I do. Um, and that's a very privileged position to be in. Um, but, uh, the, the ways that you can be got out, let's put it that way. Um, it started off with me with death threats. Um, after I made a presentation to the Evans and city council, um, internet warriors, are they real? Are they just psycho? Um, it's a crap shoot. You take your precautions.

Um, those of like you use the term, those are died down now. Um, then there's the college that gets at you. You get, uh, for all your viewers. We get in the profession, what we call the letter. Have I got your attention yet, Dr. X? Um, there's been a complaint about you. Well, that's not the standard of normal practice, um, in law. You are expected to know the nature of the complaints. Uh, you're expected to see your accuser. And that was never stated in my case. Um, my lawyer was absolutely brilliant in figuring out, but there was no complaints. It was just the college itself that it created, the concern. The consequences of that, of course, can be profound as Francis has found out. You may not just lose your ability to build a system and earn a living.

You may have your faculty position taken away from you. You may have your hospital privileges taken away from you. And those are all a bit different because at least there's some kind of a process of the colleges, although it is the star chamber in essence, um, you know, you're expected to say, yes, the Earth is flat. Can I go now? Um, that's the essence of otherwise we will bankrupt you, have I got your attention yet. Um, you know, there are all kinds of ways of getting at you, um, but there are other ways, um, you can be discredited. AP actually sent me, um, an email and it actually said, dear Mr. Hodkinson, uh, we want to debunk you. They actually use those precise words. We want to debunk you. And then there's the final indignity that, um, we as physicians in certain institutions are being forced essentially to be vaccinated otherwise we will lose our privileges. We won't be able to operate or whatever, particularly in the States, rampant, rampant in the States. So that's how they can get at you.

Dr. Roger Hodkinson: Um, the net result of that is fear. Um, the general public should know that, uh, when you get that letter, um, it certainly gets your attention because we all know the consequences of what they could do to you, um, and it's very expensive to challenge it. So, physicians are basically being forced into a decision. Is it income or is it ethics? Which goes first? Um, do I stand by my traditional ethics or do I follow the new ethics that the government are imposing on me? What a terrible choice. First, do no harm, informed consent. Am I going to stand up and be counted like we've done? The four merry men here? Um, or are we just going to go with the flow? And sadly, most of my colleagues are going with the flow. They're simply shutting up. They've been silenced. And what's the consequence of that? For society, it's tragic because we as physicians, with that respected title that comes with it, huge responsibility of not just following those ethics, but representing our patients above anyone else. We put society first. Um, the result of that has been the general public have been denied any counter narrative to support their gut feelings that this is something unreasonable and unsupported, not very clever, whatever. Um, so that's been the consequence of that general oppression: radio silence, um, for the general population. And it's resulted in a very Orwellian world. That word's been mentioned, I think by Francis. Um, and by the way, I have a t-shirt that says 'COVID 19-84.' I think that says it all.

Dr. Sam Dubé: Chris had a great t-shirt too. Something about being a one-year into the two-week lockdown or something, Chris?

Dr. Roger Hodkinson: Because in this Orwellian world, um, this upside-down world where, what the colleges call facts are actually hearsay. Where cases are no such thing. Cases in medicine, for people that are listening are people that are sick in front of you. We don't call someone who has a strand of mRNA in their snot a case. No, those are not cases. Those are simply 99% of the time in many provinces of this country, they're false positive results. Um, the word "safe" is being grotesquely misused. A single word with four letters without any qualifications whatsoever on every billboard, telling everyone this is safe. And if that's not the grossest distortion of the whole thing, everyone in the game knows that this is an experimental vaccine that is totally unsafe that was introduced under the predicate of this being a global emergency, which it certainly was not.

I would agree with John that initially there was concerns that this may be true, but there again, you see, um, Neil Ferguson's Armageddon projections, which have been wrong serially by orders of magnitude in the past; the first job of any serious medical officer of health worth the title, which is highly questionable, should be to do due diligence on the projections. That was never done anywhere internationally, and it could have been done very quickly. And if they'd done it quickly, which was their obligation, they would have realized that there was no justification for all these mandates. Another abuse of language: "imbalance." Those of you that have been following the CDC and the incidence of myocarditis following vaccination in young men, the CDC have called that an "imbalance." You're damn right, it's an imbalance. It's the CDC that's imbalanced. They've been imbalanced from the get-go. There's nothing imbalanced about myocarditis in young men. It can destroy your cardiac reserve and give you cardiac failure decades later. Oh, how convenient: decades later when Fauci will be dead and buried. God bless him. So, that distortion of facts and language has been going on, um, knowingly, culpably.

Dr. Sam Dubé: Oh, we, uh, have, uh, just an internet issue here. Roger, if you can hear me, you've frozen. Hopefully it'll come back in a moment. Yes, John

John Carpay, Esq.: I can just interject on...

Dr. Sam Dubé: Absolutely.

John Carpay, Esq.: ...On one or two points while we wait for Roger's, uh, technology thing to resolve itself. You mentioned myocarditis, uh, in children and young adults. Uh, last night I had dinner with a Calgary physician and in respect of distorting language uh, he told me that, uh, that now some of the media and certain people in the medical establishment are talking about a mild case of myocarditis. And this physician told me, and I take it to be true, I'm the only non-doctor on the panel, but he said there is no such thing as a mild case. It's a destruction of heart tissue. It's going to have a lifelong negative impact. But they're dressing that up that, well, some people are experiencing a mild case of myocarditis, um, and the abuse of safety. There's this presupposition that lockdowns are safe. No, it is not. And I don't think you need to be a doctor to recognize it is not safe to force people into loneliness and isolation. And, uh, on pain of a $2,000 tickets, tell them it's illegal to celebrate Christmas or Thanksgiving or a birthday with family members. Uh, even before lockdowns there there's abundant medical and scientific literature on the harmful effects of loneliness and isolation on people.

Uh, so, safety is singular. You've got to agree with lockdowns because, uh, I would argue that lockdowns are not safe. And I think this became apparent already in the month of May. By May of 2020, two months into this, is very clear from the death stats that this is, uh, in line with a bad annual flu. Uh, again, I mentioned the Asian flu of 1957, Hong Kong flu of 1968. Absolutely, it's serious. It should be taken seriously.

Uh, we should try to, uh, protect the vulnerable, uh, take proper precautions to help people in the nursing homes. Uh, but, but to continue with locking down the entire population, um, it's just not warranted. And I'll close briefly by saying there's a test under the charter. Uh, section one of the charter says that governments may violate charter rights and freedoms as long as those violations are reasonable and demonstrably justified in a free and democratic society. And the onus is on the government to justify the infringement. It is not up to the citizen. The way it's supposed to be under the charter, it's not up to the citizen that has to, uh, walk into court cap in hand and have to explain why it's bad for charter rights and freedoms to be violated. The onus is on the government to justify the violations and in, uh, Alberta and other provinces, the governments try very, very hard to not be in the situation of having to put evidence before the courts.

Uh, certainly in BC and in Alberta, uh, the governments have not put evidence before the court. In one of our BC cases, the judge accepted at face value knew everything that Dr. Bonnie Henry BC's Chief Medical Officer says, and the judge has accepted that. And there was no consideration of the evidence. Uh, in Alberta, the Kenney government, uh, we sued them in December of 2020 for an end to the lockdowns. They succeeded in, uh, getting the court's permission to delay presenting medical and scientific evidence until July of 2021, which tells you they don't have the medical and scientific evidence. If they did, they would be delighted to go into court and put all of us so-called unhinged conspiracy theorists, as Jason Kenney has referred to lockdown opponents. Uh, they would relish the opportunity to put us in our place and put the evidence in court and really show the whole world why and how these lockdown measures are scientific.

Dr. Sam Dubé: And they're not doing that. Yes, Chris, please. Actually, I wanted you to comment, Chris, because you went first earlier.

Dr. Chris Milburn: Just a few things that John and Roger talked about tweaked me to talk about something. I was asked to speak on a podcast recently about… there was a high-profile case, which you guys can read about. A young man died of meningitis who's 19. He was fit. He was healthy. He died of meningitis in Halifax. It was tragic. And truly for me, you get it pretty hard when you see people die all the time in ER, but, uh, boy, I was in tears listening. It was pretty tough. And it was pretty clear. What happened was the docs, the nurses, everybody who dealt with this young man had COVID blinders on. That was how his dad described it. They seem to only care if we had COVID or not. He was discharged very early despite his parents' best efforts to describe how ill he was. A part of the problem was they weren't allowed in because of COVID regulations. He got sent home. Ended coming back the next morning and sent out again. At that time, the dad ran and talked to a nurse he was brought in, but it was too late. He died of meningitis.

And I, uh, made a strong statement in discussing this on the podcast. And I actually kind of hinted that I think… I've been accused of spreading COVID misinformation, but what I tried to spread is actually actual data. Our Medical Officer of Health in Nova Scotia was quoted as saying "these new variants don't discriminate by age." That was his quote. And COVID discriminates by age a thousand times. It's a thousand times more dangerous for an elderly person than for a young person. So, the truth of it is that a 19-year-old healthy athlete, this guy was a Canada games athlete. He was that healthy, slim, and fit. His risk of dying of COVID is probably a hundred, 200 or 300 times less than the risk of dying in a car accident. So, the problem, I think when we have the Medical Officer of Health saying that COVID is extremely dangerous and it doesn't discriminate by age; the first statement is debatable at best, probably true for older folks, probably not true for younger folks, but the second statement is just not true.

It's actually false. It's misinforming positions. And I believe that was what probably led to what was a really real cognitive error. They were so intent on finding out if his gent had COVID or not. And so intent on all these COVID rules, keeping his parents out, that they never diagnosed him properly. And he died as a result of our medical errors. And I say our, because I'm a physician, we all make them. But this was one that I think was aided and abetted by public health and this hysteria really that's developed around this disease.

Dr. Sam Dubé: Hey, thank you so much for sharing that Chris and having heard everyone already speak and you having gone first. Is there anything else you'd like to add right now? Because I'd like to open it up for discussion?

Dr. Chris Milburn A couple of other things. Uh, I won't, I won't talk too long, but, um, I'll say something just generally, which I'll throw out because I think the other folks might want to discuss it. And uh, Dr. Christian Francis was mentioning about, uh, Soviet history and medical Lysenkoism is one of the terms that's being used for our current situation. So, Lysenkoism for anybody listening and doesn't know what it was, scientific conclusions got imposed by the government and they did such brilliant things as they decided that plants were communist and planting the seeds close together would help it grow more because they would cooperate and get more nutrients for soil in it. Of course, they had lots of crop fears and people starved. That's just one example of medical Lysenkoism. So anytime you try to impose science from the top, there's a real problem.

Just back to my own specific situation, I won't go through the gory detail, but, um, my comments that I talked about on this discussion on the radio got verbalized and mis-characterized by a reporter who asked Dr. Strang, our Medical Officer for health, what he thought of my comments uh, at a press conference. And Dr. Strang kind of retorted. He said, "He should stick to emergency medicine and I'll stick to public health."

That was a deeply disturbing statement because to me, it was symptomatic of everything that's wrong with our approach and our lack of discussion. As I say, I have an interest in public health. I'm not brilliant at it, and I don't, uh, have a degree in it, but boy, I've been reading intensely for 15 years and what I can tell you is that where you see the results of public health policies in primary care, in an emergency room, and a family practice. And for the chief medical officer of health of a province, seemingly had no interest in connecting with us on the front lines and not understanding that, boy, what we're seeing right now is really important. It's the first time we've locked down society, we have some theories on what might happen, but we don't really know yet. It might be a really good idea to listen to emergency docs, family docs, other specialists who are seeing certain conditions that they may not have seen otherwise. And I think, again, that statement that he made was so fundamentally flawed and shows, and this may be a strong word, but maybe an arrogance that somehow, he can sit in his office and make pronouncements and we can have no input. And I thought it was very disturbing.

Dr. Sam Dubé: "No input" is right as Francis found out, unfortunately. But, uh, Charles, um, you and I had a rather long discussion on your road to Kamloops and you said some things to me, um, that I really think we need to air. Um, one thing just to contextualize, I'm trained in family and sport medicine, but I don't do clinical. So, I do consultations in industry, medical devices, this sort of thing. I work with a lot of athletes. Um, but some of my rural family preceptors, my goodness, they didn't just know something about everything, they knew a lot about everything. And you have very unique perspective.

You go out there, you're rural, you're the only medical authority there. You're the only clinician there. So, in my experience I've found that rural family physicians and rural emergency docs, often one, and, same, um, as Chris would attest to as well. Um, Charles, they see everything and they somehow, they can make connections between things in ways that we don't see, uh, normally. They're very good at interconnecting things. And you spoke to a potential mechanism of action of the injury. And you mentioned to me the use of a D-dimer test, which we all know what it's for, but we're going to have to explain a little bit. Could you please speak to this a little bit and give it the relevant context and introduction please? Because I think this is really groundbreaking and important.

Dr. Charles Hoffe: Yes. Thank you. So, one of the key things that really bothered me when I started to see serious vaccine injuries in my own patients is that I had no idea what the mechanism of injury was. And therefore, as their doctor, I had no idea how to treat it. Because, as their family doctor, um, they would come to me for help and I needed to help them and I was clueless. So, this is an experiment. And I was aware that there was literally, um, what we call iatrogenic disease, medically induced disease being produced by this vaccine.

And so, I had asked this in my open letter to Dr. Bonnie Henry, our Provincial Health officer, what is the mechanism of injury and how do I treat this as these people's doctor? And of course, nobody knew. And the vaccine manufacturers had told us that the COVID spike protein does not go intravenously. It stays in the arm. The antibodies to the spike protein are produced in the arm um, and that's what we had been found. But scientists now, and Dr. Brody has actually very clearly revealed this, that only 25% of the vaccine actually stays in the arm and the rest of it... So, these vaccines are, a vast number of little messenger RNA strands.

The Moderna vaccine has 40 trillion messenger RNA molecules per vaccine dose. 40 trillion. So, these are wrapped in a little lipid capsule. The lipid capsule is to enable them to be absorbed into the cells. So, this is injected into the person's arm and their deltoid muscle of the shoulder. From there, as I mentioned, only 25% actually stays there. The rest is taken up, collected through the lymphatic system and fed into the general circulation. And so, it circulates around the entire body. And I think every doctor knows that absorption from the circulation occurs in capillary networks because that's where the blood slows right down. It's going through tiny, tiny vessels.

So, these little nano capsules containing these trillions of messenger RNA molecules are absorbed into the lining around the capillaries. What medically we call the vascular endothelium. So, these little packages are absorbed into the cells around the vessels, the packages open, the body recognizes these messenger RNA strands, um, as a gene and gets to work, making covert spike proteins.

So, in a virus, those COVID spike proteins form part of the viral capsule. But the problem is, they're not in a virus, they're in the cells around blood vessels. So, as a result, they become part of the cell wall of that cell. So, normally the cells that surround your blood vessels have to be very, very smooth to enable good and unimpeded flow of blood. But as soon as you've got all these little spike proteins that become part of the cell wall, it's now a rough surface. It's going to be like a very core sandpaper. It's what the platelets are now going to interpret as a damaged vessel. It's no longer smooth, It's rough.

So, clotting is inevitable because the platelets that come down that vessel are going to hit a rough spot and assume this must be a damaged vessel, this vessel needs to be blocked to stop the bleeding. That's how our clotting works.

So, because of this and because of the nature of this, clots are inevitable, because of these, um, spike proteins in the capillary networks. So, I set out to then try and prove this. Could this theory be correct? And so, the problem is these little clots in the capillary networks are microscopic and they are scattered, so they're not going to show on any scan. They're just too small and too scattered. They're not like the big clots that cause strokes or heart attacks. Um, they're too small and they're too scattered so how on Earth can we know if the person clotted? And the only way is with a blood test called a D-dimer. So, the D-dimer is a blood test that will show up a recent clot. It would show up an old clot, it shows up a new clot. And it doesn't tell you where the clot is. It just tells you that the clotting mechanism has been activated.

So, I have now been recruiting patients from my practice, people that have come into my office and others that have that have heard me speak about this and ask people to do this D-dimer within one week of their COVID shot and so far, and the study is ongoing, these are preliminary results, I've got 62% positive elevated D-dimer, which means that the blood clots are not rare. That's what the so-called "experts" keep telling us the clots are rare. The big ones are rare, but the small ones are clearly happening in the majority of people. 62%. Now, I'll tell you what the real concern with this is: a clotted vessel is permanently damaged. That vessel never, ever goes back to normal.

So, if this theory is correct, which it really looks like by these D-dimer results. And I'm told it has been done in Australia and it's been done in the UK and they also found elevated D-dimer. Um, and they sort of discarded the information because they said there's no clinical evidence of clots. Well, the reason is because they're microscopic and they're scattered and so, you're not going to see clinical evidence. But in fact, all of the frequent side effects of the shot, which are headache, nausea, dizziness, fatigue, could all be signs of cerebral thrombosis on a capillary level.

Literally you could be having thousands and thousands of tiny, tiny little clots in your brain that won't show on scan, but they will give you those exact symptoms. So, the concern is I have now got six people in my medical practice that cannot exert themselves the way they used to: what medically we call reduced effort tolerance. Six people who now get out of breath doing things that they could previously do without any problem. So, I believe that these people have blocked up thousands and thousands of capillaries in their lungs; these six people. I believe these people now have permanently damaged lungs because they have got… and that's why they get out of breath.

I have one fellow that used to walk two miles to my office every week for, uh, a shot for his arthritis. And he says after a quarter of a mile, he's done. In other words, his effort tolerance has reduced to one eighth of what it used to be. And so, I've sent some of these people for chest x-rays and CT scans to see what it shows. And all it shows is distorted architecture. What the radiologist's described as increased articulation. It's a very non-specific thing and it's because it's microscopic. But the concern is because these vessels are now permanently damaged in a person's lungs, when the heart tries to pump blood through all those damaged vessels, there's increased resistance trying to pump the blood through those lungs. So, those people are going to develop something called pulmonary artery hypertension, high blood pressure in the lungs. And the concern with that is that those people will probably all develop right-sided heart failure within three years and die because they now have increased vascular resistance through those lungs and lung tissue and heart tissue and brain and spinal tissue, all of that does not regenerate. In other tissues, it can regenerate: liver and kidneys and muscle and others, but there are some tissues that cannot, and so, this absolutely explains what I've seen in my patients and that's what I'm doing to prove it and my study is ongoing.

Dr. Chris Milburn I'll just, uh, just throw in that there was a journal article in JAMA cardiology about that issue that you're talking about, reduced exercise tolerance, and it just came out. I'm not sure if you've seen it.

Dr. Charles Hoffe: Right. And I should also mention that finally, an autopsy has been done on a vaccine death which showed COVID spike proteins in almost every organ in their body. So, that supports this theory of the widespread damage caused by these spike proteins. These spike proteins are toxic to our bodies, and that's why people with COVID infections get a higher risk of clotting. The same reason as people with the vaccination get higher risk of clotting. But the common factor is the COVID spike proteins. They are toxic.

Dr. Sam Dubé: And yet, the CBC issued a publication on June 13th to combat "vaccine hesitancy," where they state that there's almost no evidence for long-term side effects of the vaccine and that the spike protein is harmless, completely harmless to the Canadian people.

Dr. Chris Milburn Um, my take on that, just to say that I think the answer is we don't know the long-term side effects yet, and I think there's this war that we want to decide if there is, or there isn't. And I think there's lots of reason to be concerned and, uh, there's no reason to say that there's not going to be, or there shouldn't be other than faith. And um, science shouldn't be a religion and it should be a process of deduction, reason, hypothesis generation, which is speculating. So, I got in trouble with some people for speculating that there could be long-term side effects, but that's actually science to say, boy, this drug works in this way, I wonder if this might happen, we should look for it. That's actually, the first step of science is to speculate. And if we can't even speculate, or get shut down then we're never going to find these things out. We're never going to know.

Dr. Sam Dubé: Absolutely Francis, uh, John, please. We'd love to…

Dr. Francis Christian: Sam, um, I just keep coming back to totalitarianism and the Soviet Union because I've studied the Soviet Union and its control really, really well and in detail. And, um, some of the things that Charles said makes intuitive, pathophysiological sense. And many of the great advances in surgery and in medicine, uh, have come from people like Charles. Uh, um, whether you agree with him or not, should he not get the hearing by mainstream media, by, um, CBC science program. Here's a guy who comes up with a novel theory which is actually proving to be true. Uh, it's not peer-reviewed. That's one of the most abused terms nowadays. Uh, but, many of the great advances in science and medicine have been from small series of patients like Charles is describing. So, what we are saying is, you don't have to agree with us, but give Charles a chance to put this out there. It might save lives and that's not happening. And I got to tell you, uh, and your viewers Sam, you know, people say, "Oh, okay, this is a temporary phase. And you know, it'll pass." Uh, but that's not the experience of totalitarian regimes.

Uh, and I'm reading this now from the Council of the People's Commissars after the communist revolution and in the Soviet Union. Decree on the press; November 9th, 1917. So, it says here "Publications can be proscribed temporarily or permanently only by the decision of the council of people's commissars." That's exactly what's happening now. The commissars now, uh, are the mainstream media, uh, the people who run CDC, uh, and the big Silicon Valley giants. So, uh, it's only by the decision of these guys that you can actually, uh, publish what you're saying. And then it says in the same ordinance, "The present ordinance is of a temporary nature and will be repealed by a special decree as soon as normal conditions of social life set in." And we all know Sam that the Soviet system of tyranny lasted not a little time, but 70 years, 70 years. And you know, this whole thing they're doing now with dividing society, with the vaccine certificates that's been called passports. Whatever you call them. Uh, that was a very good tactic of the Soviet Union too. The human heart hasn't really changed.

We can slip into tyranny, um, without us even knowing it. And, uh, in the Soviet Union, it was children who were the easiest, uh, targets for propaganda. Uh, since we had to attend state run schools where teachers were fired if they didn't tow the party line, if they were for example, telling kids about, uh, about Christianity or Judaism or any religion. Uh, and then, this is all on record. People can actually check this out. Schools had outings on Sunday mornings and children who admitted to attending Church received poorer marks. Because of the anti-religious tone of education in the Soviet Union, frequently students mocked other students for believing religious things. So, uh, what the government is doing now is dividing people and saying, "Oh, you are un-vaccinated so you don't need to come near me." They're turning also children against parents. Um, and that is an old tactic too. It was used in the Soviet Union. And, uh, this creeping tyranny will be upon us soon if we don't wake up.

And again, we physicians, we scientists, we know, and we continue to believe that throughout history, it's opposing views, vigorous debate, and openness to new ideas. These have been the bedrock of scientific progress and any major advance in science has been arrived at by practitioners, um, not towing the line, but vigorously questioning official narratives and following a different path in the pursuit of truth. And these have always been the methods of science. All this is under assault and, um, your show Sam is… I was reminded again from the Soviet era. Uh, in 1946, the BBC, which now unfortunately is another arm of government. But in 1946, the BBC started broadcasting radio service to Soviet citizens. Uh, messages of freedom. Uh, the voice of America did that, the Deutsche Welle did that. And, um unsurprisingly, The Kremlin was not happy with the Western media beaming messages of liberty, and they started blocking the radio frequencies. Um, if Canadians don't recognize that there are not just similarities, but really frightening similarities to what is going on now, uh, the totalitarianism will be upon them before they know it. And again, from Soviet history and Nazi history. Uh, it is not the practice of tyrannical regimes to take away all your freedoms in one fell sweep.

They take a little bit at a time and a little bit at a time. And then by the time the people wake up and people do wake up, because the quest for human freedom and liberty can never be suppressed forever. But by the time they wake up, it may be too late. And, uh, Charles' little scientific study is a perfect example. In the Soviet Union, he would have probably been sent to the Gulag or something for, uh, opposing the official Soviet narrative. What we are saying is give all voices a chance, hear all voices. It might actually save some lives.

Dr. Chris Milburn I'd just like to add, there's a great quote from Thomas Paine who said, "He who dares not offend, cannot speak the truth." And I think that is a true message with all of the things we discussed in society. It's being brought now into the scientific realm where the colleges have sort of a defined stepping out of the narrative. And as our Nova Scotia College has said, anything but unanimity will be considered an offense and we cannot speak the truth if we're constantly worried about stepping on someone's toes, hurting their feelings, or making them feel bad that they might be wrong. That's just necessary with everything in science, particularly with science. It's actually the basis of science.

Dr. Roger Hodkinson: If I could comment…

Dr. Sam Dubé: Yes, I'd like to give Roger a chance.

Dr. Roger Hodkinson: I'm sorry. When I was frozen, I saw the look on my face. It looked like something that, um, Fox news might've put on about, um, Hillary Clinton.

Dr. Sam Dubé: I wasn't going to comment, but you went there. You went there, Roger. I tried calling you. I tried calling you three times, so at least we could get you on speaker phone with my microphone, but you were so busy coming back so we're so glad to have you back.

Dr. Roger Hodkinson: Charles. Um, I completely concur. I've been saying that myself. There's no way of checking on micro-vascular thrombosis. And the true incidents of these events, I think you're demonstrating quite clearly, is much more prevalent than we could initially think. Those results are also being replicated in Germany, by the way, Charles, with the Doctors for COVID Ethics. Um, Sucharit Bhakdi is doing a similar study. Um, so yeah. That's one point. What I wanted to end with, uh, my soliloquy, was, this is the most sinister thing to me. Um, these medical officers of health that are practicing medicine on society, they are governed by the same ethics that the four of us are. And the colleges are supposed to be managing how individual physicians live up to those ethics. We're not allowed to do more hurt… we can't do more harm than good. Um, we can't cut off the wrong leg. Um, we can't give people pills without telling them about the complications. We can't do any of that. And yet that is precisely what government is doing. And it is the role of the college not to protect us just from doctors who are pedophiles. It's the role of the college to protect the public from doctors in general.

And if they see government doing terrible things to the population, which is strictly medical malpractice, I call the colleges out right here and now. Instead of protecting the public good, you are killing the public because by suppressing information, you are contributing to the absence of informed consent. You're contributing to the protests. You're obstructing protests about lockdowns; all of which have serious medical consequences, including death. And so, I call every college across this country out right here on this program. You are despicable, you are doing exactly what you're supposed not to do. You wouldn't tolerate it from the four of us. And so, you should not tolerate it from government. You should be banging the table. What are you doing? Why are you doing this? It is unconscionable and its medical malpractice on the most grotesque scale sanctioned by the state. Colleges have become the enforcers of government. They forced us as physicians to put income ahead of ethics. Despicable choices that are being presenting to us. And I call them all out. Do to me as you will, but you've lost your way. And I despise the lot of you.

Dr. Chris Milburn Can I add onto that? And then what I've been disturbed by is, um, I think the college has suffered from the mission creep of the woke and they're responsible, and John can correct me on this, but I think they're tasked with enforcing the safe and reasonable practice of medicine, right? That's their mandate. But what they've now done is gone beyond that. And like I say, in that chilling statement they sent out to us in Nova Scotia, they're there to enforce unanimity and to make sure that nobody argues with public health and to make sure that no physician can, uh, use any drug off-label, um, all these things which pre-COVID seemed perfectly acceptable. The college just felt that it's there to, um, uh, mandate unanimity of view and it is a very communist ideas as, uh, Francis has already said.

Dr. Roger Hodkinson: Let me comment on that, if I may, Chris, the hypocrisy of that. If out of one side of their mouths, these colleges and governments are saying, this is an emergency, therefore we need an emergency vaccine, et cetera, et cetera. We know it's not an emergency, but let's take that at face value for a minute. Let's say it really was an emergency, which it's glaringly not; if you're saying that out of one side of your mouth, you can't say out of the other side of your mouth that "I'm going to specifically prohibit physicians from prescribing agents that are safe," hydroxychloroquine and ivermectin, demonstrably safe and which, probably, in the opinion of many physicians, will save lives. They're wanting it both ways. You can't have it both ways. If it's that big an emergency, you've got to take the dogs off physicians and let us practice medicine. Stick to your knitting and let us practice medicine because we've got people dying in front of us. What are they saying to those people that appear at an emergency department who don't have a PO too low enough? They're saying, "come back when you're blue." Well, that may be too late. That could have been stopped by ivermectin or hydroxychloroquine and to a substantial degree.

Peter McCullough believes that of the 600,000 deaths in the United States that may be half a million of them could have been saved by people being given ivermectin, hydroxychloroquine or some cocktail there of to go home with, instead of coming back, when you're blue. That's like New York's sending COVID positive patients, um, back to nursing homes, massively culpable. You see at every level, anyone listening to this, I want to get across to you all, at every single level there's been culpability, whether it's from about Fauci at the get go, to the colleges now to vaccine passports, a two-class society. Do we ever demand that HIV patients have a tattoo on their forehead? No, we don't. It's against human rights. And one other thing, the letter that, it's called the messenger actually, the communication that came out from my college, didn't just say, "Dr. Hodkinson, your opinions are hearsay, and we have the facts," if that's not Orwellian itself, but they also went on to saying the same communication, "and we suggest that you do not discuss this with your neighbors" in print. How Orwellian can that be? Are they going to determine what we're thinking next?

Dr. Chris Milburn: I received and, uh, John may not be aware of this because it was dealt with, by one of his other lawyers, but when I was looked into for my editorial a year and a half ago, where I committed the crime of calling people criminals if they had done something against the law, uh, the college trolled my Facebook and I had written a strongly worded but I thought reasonable, um, argument against Bill M103, the anti-xenophobia bill on the grounds that criminalizing the criticism of religion in Canada is anti-democratic and just a terrible thing to do. And I had actually gotten a note from the college saying, the actual note said, "We just wanted to check your thinking on this." So, we're already there. We're already there. The colleges are already the thought police apparently.

Dr. Roger Hodkinson: And they're about to send Francis off to Gulag because Francis you're really not well, are you? You need help. We have a special psychiatric hospital for you, Dr. Christian.

Dr. Francis Christian: I've got to tell you, um, in the comments and there are hundreds of thousands of comments in the thousands of things whether recording is now available, um, that there are many comments that talk about those words being bone chilling or stomach turning and so on. I've got to tell you when I was there, the words, those words, uh, were very disturbing, but they were not bone chilling because I knew… You can actually check this out because you can, you can see the transcripts of the tribunals the Nazi and the Soviet regimes, set up for academics. They went after academics first because…. [**inaudible 45 :11**]

Dr. Sam Dubé: My apologies. I had a video ready for us. Sorry about that, guys. Can you hear me, okay?

Dr. Francis Christian: Yeah. I'm sorry. Did I cut-off?

Dr. Sam Dubé: No, okay. I had a video prepared to use and it started playing spontaneously so I apologize for that.

Dr. Francis Christian: That's all right. Well, uh, I was just saying that, uh, there are comments that call that exchange with me, uh, anything from bone chilling to stomach turning and so on. And because I had studied the transcripts of the Soviet tribunals that were set up for academics, uh, I was very disturbed when I heard those, but it wasn't bone chilling. You can check it out. In fact, there are even some videos of these tribunals, uh, that are basically, uh, this talking down to academics, de-platforming them, smearing them and then finally, sending them to, uh, uh, to the Gulag or, uh, to concentration camps.

Uh, I make the point in that recording that I'm not accusing the people there of being Nazis or Soviet agents. But if you look at the proceedings of how they went after the academics, the parallels are very, very, very close. Um, things like "Francis, you're an intelligent man, but you are using your intelligence for wrong things."

Uh, you know, getting together with the wrong people. Uh, these are directly... these transcripts can be found almost word for word from those Nazi tribunals that went after the academics, because they knew if they capture the ideas in the academy, they would, they could propagate and promulgate their totalitarian rule much more easily.

And so, they went after the academics first. They went after physicians. But I have to tell you, uh, Sam, that, you know, freedom and liberty can never be suppressed forever. And when the people wake up from this Orwellian nightmare and science is once more restored to its rightful place in our academies, uh, there will be a reckoning.

There'll be reckoning based on whether there've been criminal acts committed. Now this is not, uh, you know, I'm not being rhetorical or dramatic. Uh, I'm just taking from history.

Uh, the Nuremberg Trials were basically, uh, a very broad set of trials, but the Nuremberg Code was a set of rules drafted in the aftermath of the atrocities perpetrated within the Nazi concentration camps. And in these camps, horrific medical experiments were performed on inmates without consent. And the Nuremberg Code expressly forbids the imposition of any kind of intervention without informed consent.

Now, one of our colleagues in Trial Site News had very scholarly article on how every one of those 10 Nuremberg Codes are now being violated now.

So, when the reckoning comes, you, the colleges, the authorities may be found guilty of crimes against humanity. Do you really want to be on that side of history? So, I make this appeal to my colleagues, to physicians, scientists, surgeons, uh, specialists, everywhere. Uh, if you think there's something going on that is wrong, but are just going with the flow, that cannot be an excuse. The Nuremberg Trials actually, uh, ruled on that. You can't say that you're just following orders. It's not an excuse. And of course, John is the scholar here and he can tell you a little bit more on this. But, uh, just following orders is not an excuse.

Blocking ivermectin which is actually being done now. I, uh, wanted to get ivermectin for, uh, close friends of mine, and there is no ivermectin available in all of Saskatchewan. The government, big pharma is blocking ivermectin. So that, uh, like you said, Sam, if you have good early treatment, as Roger pointed out so eloquently, if you have good early treatment, there is no emergency. It takes out the wind from their sails. They cannot then push the vaccine. And the blocking of ivermectin is another potential crime against humanity. Hundreds of thousands of lives could have been saved. What are these people thinking? So, my colleagues, this is my appeal to you. Come on the right side of history. If there's something, if the voice of conscience within you is say, "Uh, I'm doing something wrong. I have to question this narrative." Now is the time to do it. Uh, another few months may be too late

Dr. Roger Hodkinson: Especially as children. And now in this swing.

Dr. Francis Christian: Exactly.

Dr. Roger Hodkinson: It could be the most horrendous consequence of this madness. If in fact, I hope I'm wrong, everyone obviously does. But if there are fertility issues as a consequence of this, it could be the most grotesque mistake ever made in medical history. And we don't know. Anyone listening, medical trials had done for one reason and one reason only because you don't know what you don't know. If we knew what could happen, we wouldn't do them. It's to find out the unexpected and lo and behold, six months into this game, we're finding all kinds of complications coming out of the woodwork. Totally predictable. The trials should have been extended for a significant period of time. Typically, five to seven years for a vaccine, especially a vaccine that's introduced with new technology. That was not done.

Dr. Chris Milburn I don't want this to be too much of a love in, so I'll push back a little bit. I'll say that I don't have a big problem with, um, people putting a vaccine out into a big trial like this. I think this is a significant disease for older people, and if people were informed and chose to be vaccinated, that's okay by me. I'm fine with that.

My problem is it wasn't presented as, "We haven't studied this well yet, and we don't know the long-term consequences because this hasn't been out long-term, but, so by definition, we don't know." It wasn't presented that way to people. It was presented as, "This has been well studied, well tested. We know it's good and everybody should get it." Boom. Done. And so, I don't look at it as a bad thing that this was attempted. I look at it as a bad thing of how it was rolled out, how it was described.

Dr. Roger Hodkinson: Let me address that, Chris. If they are saying that this is an emergency of so grotesque proportions, that it warrants the introduction of a warp speed vaccine, that's not being tested anywhere close to what it should have been, then here's another exposure that they have.

If you were going to do that with such potential, for horrible things happening, then you are obligated as government to put in place, right from the very get go, a very efficient monitoring system for what is going wrong. And that was not done. It's not even done now.

I was really struck by hearing Dr. Patrick say, um, a few days ago that here we have a very caring physician who's aware of the adverse reactions and all the rest of it.

He submitted six adverse reactions. Five of them were rejected. They were rejected because he didn't have the lot number of the vaccine vial. Well, hello bureaucrats, that was a few days, a couple of weeks ago. Of course, he doesn't have it. But the net result was that those events didn't get in the database.

Dr. Chris Milburn I totally agree. And so, as a physician in active clinical practice, and I have to be careful, I don't want to violate any patient confidentiality, but I've seen a couple of, uh, certainly what looked like serious vaccine reactions just recently. And it's very onerous.

So, a few things; firstly, it wasn't at all clear to my group, um, or our physician group, what should be reported and what shouldn't. My understanding is that anything that could potentially be a vaccine side effect should be reported because the whole point is to generate data. Yes, sure. It might be coincidence that person got vaccinated and walked out of the building, a metre fell on their head. It's probably coincidence. But there are many of these things, it's only through the viewing statistical trends that we'll find out. So, my understanding was we should pretty much report everything. We had seen a lady who had a blood clotting issue several days after the vaccine.

Note, that could have been coincidental because we see them every day in emerge, but it wasn't reported cause the doctors discussed and said, no, she was probably high risk anyway and probably it would have happened anyway. It wasn't reported. And I do believe it wasn't and I suggested it probably should be for data keeping purposes.

But just recently, uh, two days ago, uh, I had a very serious what looked like a vaccine reaction. And I went to report it as my second one and I was reminded how onerous the form is. It's incredible. It's a five-page form. It's got all this fine print. It would be enough to put anyone who wasn't very serious about reporting off doing it. And many of the questions they asked, like I say, were completely irrelevant to what I wanted to report and it would've just taken me huge amounts of time. And in the end, I did a kind of a messed-up job of filling it in best I could in the midst of a busy clinic day and I sent it off and I will follow up on it and make sure that it got filed properly. But boy, you have to be very, uh... you have to b e very focused and determined to get that, uh, reported. It should be easy. This should have been set up well ahead of time, it should have been well explained and it should be easy for doctors if we're going to get good reporting.

Dr. Roger Hodkinson: And for people listening, who are not familiar with the reporting system, Canada is in the dark ages. It's an abysmal system. The ones in the States in Britain are somewhat better, but even in the States... look, anyone listening, we've had 6,000 deaths in the States over three months because the three months behind in reporting the data. We've had 6,000 deaths in the states attributed to the vaccine. Now, not validated, but that number is vastly greater than all the deaths that have ever been recorded as due to vaccinations over the last 30 years.

It's that scale of death. And a lot of those deaths are occurring in old people. Look, they can't have it both ways. That that scale of death after vaccination in a normal clinical trial would have shut it down within weeks and yet it's still going on. The biggest experiment in medical history is currently underway.

John Carpay, Esq.: Now, one aspect that I found interesting with the discussion of vaccine deaths, uh, it's like the, uh, the pro lock down forces, uh, so to speak are now using a similar argument to what anti-lockdown people have been saying in the past year, which is that, uh, COVID is not having a big impact on life expectancy, population life expectancy from, uh, years of life lost analysis. Uh, this is another thing that distinguishes it from the Spanish flu of 1918, where people in their twenties, thirties, and forties were dying and in huge numbers. So, the impact on life expectancy is not huge.

Uh, I read a column in the *National Post* by one of the mainstream media, pro-lockdown pro-vaccine, and, uh, it's an interesting passage. It refers to a study in Norway, uh, and says, "Well, but all these vaccine deaths are taking place in nursing homes and people die in nursing homes all the time. And so, this is not really having a big impact on the life expectancy, uh, because most of these vaccine deaths are in, uh, elderly people who are in poor health, who are going to die pretty soon anyways." And it was, it was just interesting to see that flip.

Where I see the whole thing going, just to move briefly into the legal-political aspect of it. Uh, I think what we're very likely to see is a lifting of most of the... eventually. Today, July 1st in Alberta, we've got supposedly this great reopening taking place. Um, but what I foresee is a lifting of some of the, uh, lockdown measures. So, relaxing or a repeal of the masking bylaws and social distancing limits on numbers of people permitted into houses of worship, et cetera, et cetera, et cetera. The big scary thing is the vaccine passport. It's already there in Manitoba, where there is an immunization card and immediately with the rollout of the immunization card, the government already announced that those who have it, those who have the immunization card will have greater privileges to be able to visit their loved ones in a nursing home or to visit their loved ones in hospital. Uh, Trudeau announced within the past two weeks that come this fall, uh, international travel will only be available to those who are immunized. So, that's already an announcement of intention.

There has been no law passed, uh, to my knowledge, to that effect. So, what we are rapidly heading towards is uh, two classes of citizens. First class citizens who've got their proof that they've had two vaccines, and the second-class citizens who may very well be denied their right to go to a movie theatre, or a shopping mall, or sending their kids to a public school. Uh, it's very rapidly moving towards, uh, two classes of citizenship with, with a *de facto* persecution against the non-vaccinated in the same way that in a totalitarian regime, uh, you've got the bad guys, like in the Soviet Union, the bad guys are the capitalists, the bourgeoisie. Uh, in Nazi Germany, the bad guys were the Jews. And uh, this is what we're heading towards with totalitarianism, because there is there's one truth and there's one villain and there's one solution and everybody has to get with the program. But I want to conclude my remarks briefly on a positive note, which is that we still have a lot of free speech. Uh, Sam, I would say don't post this to YouTube, but post it to Rumble, somewhere else.

Dr. Sam Dubé: I'm going to try BitChute and Rumble.

John Carpay, Esq.: YouTube would take this down in seconds.

Dr. Sam Dubé: Absolutely.

John Carpay, Esq.: So, we still have our free speech rights. We still have the ability to organize, to create organizations. There are various doctors' groups, which I think is wonderful. In this particular time in human history. In resisting totalitarianism, it is the voices of the medical doctors that are the most important because you have a credibility that non-doctors do not have. I could say things that are medically true or medically accurate, but nobody cares. I'm not a doctor. If you say things that are medically true and medically accurate, people sit up and take notice. And this is what's so upsetting to the authorities. They know that when a doctor questions lockdowns, or it just raises questions about the vaccines, they know how powerful that is because people look up to doctors and rightfully so. Um, so I think the good news is if we continue to speak truth and continue to organize and be involved in various organizations, there are so many doctors' groups. I couldn't even list them with accuracy. They're out there Canadian wide and internationally. So, we just have to speak truth to power, keep on fighting, keep on displaying courage and, uh, don't give up. And, uh, that's the way to resist the tyranny: to continue to speak the truth.

Dr. Chris Milburn Um, just to comment, I do worry about this two-tiered citizenship that we're heading into. That's a great concern. The other concern that I have is sort of a broader concern that we've now kind of, uh, made it… It's become okay for, for one unelected, unaccountable public health official to mandate all kinds of things in our lives, the details of our lives. And I picture this dystopian future where we wake up in the morning and before we do anything, before we get out of bed, step in the bathtub, take any risk, we have to look and go to the government app and say, "how full are the hospitals today? What am I allowed to do? Well, I was going to go on a bike ride with my friends, but the ICU is full, I can't do that. I was going to take a bath today, but if I fell and hit my head." And, of course I'm using an extreme version of it, but we've kind of okayed that kind of thinking in our head.

The healthcare system, uh, is there to serve Canadians, but the healthcare system being full, which it is all the time is, it was never meant to give the government a mandate to shut down our lives and shut down our choices. And as a collective, I think we've accepted that and thought that somehow that's okay. And I'm really just deeply disturbed by that fundamental shift in thinking that I've felt over the last year or more.

Dr. Sam Dubé: Huge, huge red flag too. So, guys, we can definitely continue talking, but I think, uh, it's time to try to wrap this up. Uh, would you be amenable to doing this again sometime because there are many more questions that I would like to address with your distinguished company? Uh, John of course included. We need your legal expertise. We need your insight, my friend. So, um, any final thoughts, Charles, uh, Francis and Roger? Charles?

Dr. Charles Hoffe: Um, no, I don't think I have any. I just absolutely agree with what everybody said. I think we've highlighted very many critical, um, red flags and, um, so no, I don't think I have anything else to add.

Dr. Sam Dubé: Okay. Francis?

Dr. Francis Christian: Um, I don't either. I just want to reiterate my appeal to the public and to my colleagues, uh, wake up from the creeping dystopian darkness that is approaching. If you don't, it may be too late.

Dr. Sam Dubé: Thank you, Francis. Roger?

Dr. Roger Hodkinson: Believe nothing you're being told. It's all a pack of lies. They're distorting the truth at every juncture. Rely upon your own good head because you've got it straight. There's something smelly in the state of Denmark. You've got it dead right. Hug people, shake hands, let your children see your faces. Try and live life normally because when the truth of this comes out in what are called books, they can't get rid of those heads will roll. There'll be blood in the gutter. And hopefully we'll have learned great lessons from this.

Dr. Sam Dubé: On that note, gentlemen, I want to thank you so much for your participation, Dr. Chris Milburn, Dr. Charles Hoffe, Dr. Francis Christian, Dr. Roger Hodgkinson. And of course, John Carpay Esquire. Your participation in this is so appreciated. And, uh, I want to thank our viewers for tuning in, and we will do this again sometime. So, spread the word, ladies and gentlemen. Please spread the word and be eternally vigilant and be safe. So, I want to thank you so much and on behalf of all of us here, Happy Canada Day.

Dr. Charles Hoffe: Thanks, Sam.
   [**Crosstalk 02:06:33**]

AUDIO [from a Saskatchewan provincial hearing]

Male Voice 1: Morning Francis.

Dr. Francis Christian: Good morning. Good morning.

Male Voice 1: Good. Thank you for attending. Um, I just wanted to, um, let you know who was all at the meeting, I'm sure, you know, Dr. Susan Shaw.

Dr. Francis Christian: Yes, I do.
[Inaudible 02:07:25]

Male Voice 1: We also have Dr., uh, Dean Preston Smith, obviously the dean of medicine and myself, and, uh, we'd like to thank you for, uh, attending this meeting. Uh, and this meeting is, uh, to inform you of a number of issues that have arisen, uh, regarding, uh, your recent engagement as it relates to COVID-19 response in, um, in Saskatchewan. Um, I am, uh, in my role as provincial heads, um, I would, uh, I'm going to inform you of a letter that will be sent, uh, and the contents of a letter that will be sent to you immediately following the meeting, uh, not only, uh, by email, but I'll do it by registered mail, uh, as well. Uh, so, um, and so we'll also have response from Dr. Susan Shaw and, um, Dean Smith. So, uh, without any further ado, Francis, uh, in my role as provincial head of the department surgery, I'm notifying you that the college of medicine has received information that you are engaging in activities designed to discourage and prevent children and adolescents from receiving COVID-19 vaccinations contrary to the recommendations and pandemic response efforts of Saskatchewan and Canadian, uh, public health authorities. In addition to questions regarding your media and social media activity relating to vaccination, uh, it is of significant concern that your activity… you actively participated in recent demonstration out of Saskatoon High school.

And that this demonstration was designed to persuade youth to decline vaccination. This information raises serious questions as to whether you are engaging in unprofessional conduct contrary to individual and public safety. In light of this information and investigation by the college of medicine, we'll proceed under the procedures manual for medical faculty. Uh, I will be sending you a copy by email with the letter of the procedures manual to enclose that in a package, but due to the serious nature of these concerns, uh, your academic responsibilities are temporarily and immediately suspended pending the outcome of the investigation. Uh, that also means that any… and there will be no involvement clinically or academically with any learners, whether it be students or residents. Um, this also includes suspension of your academic responsibilities as quality improvement and patient safety director and director of surgical humanities.

Uh, you are entitled to an appeal to the academic clinical relations committee complaints and appeals subcommittee for review of this decision to suspend your academic responsibilities. Uh, you should know that the College of Medicine is not suspending the payment for services you would otherwise have received under your ACFE during this investigation period and the College of Medicine will be in touch with you regarding next steps, uh, in this investigation.

Maybe, uh, at this point just to reiterate, so at this point in time, um, your academic responsibilities are temporarily and immediately suspended pending the outcome of the investigation. I will be, uh be speaking with Dr. John Shaw, uh, the ADL and division head of general surgery on how this affects your, your current duties.

Um, I'm fully aware of the issues regarding, um, a learner involvement with the ACS and trauma service and we'll work through this. Uh, obviously you'll be looking after your own personal elective patients, uh, but from a learner perspective, uh, both clinical and academic, uh, activities are suspended as and as mentioned, um, your responsibilities as director for quality improvement, patient safety and surgical humanities. I'll maybe stop there and, uh, ask, uh, Dr. Susan Shaw to make further comments.

Dr. Francis Christian: Um, can I just say something here, please? Can I say something? On what basis are you essentially not allowing me to work?

Dr. Susan Shaw: You're allowed to work, Francis. You're not allowed to use your academic faculty appointments, um, based on the suspension. That's all within the letter and that will be a part of the investigation and the review.

Dr. Francis Christian: My role in the hospital is an academic role

Dr. Susan Shaw: And it is suspended at this time.

Dr. Francis Christian: So, what you're saying is I don't… Basically, you're not letting me work.

Dr. Susan Shaw: No, that is not true. That is not correct. And I will let you know the outcome of the next part, which is for me to share with you. We're not impacting your privileges. We have not impacted your license. We have not impacted your ability to work. But I do need to let you know that based on the letter within your language, I'm giving you 90 days' notice of termination without cause of the contractual relationship between the health authority and yourself under your language of clause 5.2 which was signed between us.

Dr. Francis Christian: One of you has just spoken.

Dr. Susan Shaw: I have given you notice that the agreement will terminate on, September 21, 2021. Your privileges at this time are not impacted. However, this notice is given without prejudice and we retain, uh, all of the rights, powers, privileges, remedies, and or defenses which the SHA currently has within the privilege system outlined within the bylaws. These are all at this time expressly reserved. You remain able to practice as a surgeon, after September 21st, but not in a contractual relationship with the health authority. You will receive a written copy of this by email and by registered mail immediately following this meeting.

Dr. Francis Christian: What is this? Why are you meeting with me if you don't allow me to speak?

Dr. Susan Shaw: This to give you the information around your...

Dr. Francis Christian: You can send me a letter. I know your faces really well. So, I there's no need.... if you don't let me speak.

Dr. Susan Shaw: You can speak now.

Dr. Francis Christian: This is exactly the problem, isn't it? You're censoring people, not allowing people to speak. You're not allowing people to protect the vulnerable. It is not only a, uh, very unprofessional thing. It is also contrary to informed consent and the basic principles of medicine. You are violating all of those principles. Did you know, by the way, any of you, that the WHO has asked that children not be vaccinated?

Dr. Susan Shaw: That is not accurate. That is certainly not accurate Francis. We are not here to debate the merits of the position, we're here to inform you of decisions at the health authority...

Dr. Francis Christian: And you're not letting me speak.

Dr. Susan Shaw: …Is required to take at this time, based on the current situation that you have entered into based on the policies and procedures.

Dr. Francis Christian: The WHO has suspended, and, uh, in fact then…

[crosstalk 02:15:06]

Dr. Francis Christian: It's not a debate. I'm just telling you the statement. The statement was put out, uh, on Monday morning and the WHO has stated that children should not be vaccinated from 12 to 18. And anybody less than 18 should not be vaccinated. You guys claim that you listen to the WHO,

Male Voice 1: I would like to speak…

Dr. Francis Christian: You've spoken now for 90% of the time, so it's only fair that I can speak as well.

Male Voice 2: So, Francis, I would like to speak, I haven't spoken yet.

Dr. Francis Christian: You've basically read out some indictments against me. These were exactly the sort of panels that were set up in the Soviet Union and in Nazi Germany against academics. These are the types of panels anyway. Uh, I'm not saying that you're Nazis or Soviets, but it's, it's really disturbing. Isn't it? Because I called for informed consent. Informed consent from parents and children, uh, I am essentially not being allowed to practice and to teach residents and to teach students. This is disturbing, dystopian, and it's just not acceptable.

Male Voice 2: So, Francis, as I said, I'd like to speak. Um, the purpose of this meeting is to inform you of the actions that the College of Medicine has taken at this time and likewise the SHA has taken. And, uh, certainly the provincial head is here because he represents both organizations to the department of surgery. I am here as is Susan to support the provincial head. The decision with regards to the suspension of your faculty appointment is a temporary pending an investigation. And you will have your opportunity to make your argument. That is not the purpose of this meeting. This meeting is, is, is simply to inform you of the decision made, uh, after due consideration by the College of Medicine and, uh, the SHA.

We recognize, um, this decision may be distressing to you and, uh, want to emphasize, um, to you, uh, the need um, to, uh, first of all, look to the contract and look to the policy and procedures on medical faculty appointment to see the avenues that are available to you as this process unfolds. That will likely include the need for your own, uh, advice in determining best paths. And there are people in legal, uh, representation that can advise you as you follow your way through these procedures. Uh, and the second thing that is really important to me is that you do take care of yourself through this process. This is a stressful process and an unfortunate process that has been made necessary, by the actions today. But it is still stressful and difficult. So, in that realm, there are many supports available to you or, and particularly the physician health program.

Dr. Francis Christian: I just have to say something.

Male Voice 2: I'm speaking. And I will finish speaking and then you can speak.

Dr. Francis Christian: I have to say that I'm not stressed at all.

Male Voice 2: I will finish speaking and then you can speak.

Dr. Francis Christian: I'm not distressed at all.

Male Voice 2: I understand.

Dr. Francis Christian: You don't have to shout over me.

Male Voice 2: That's your choice, but I simply want to make sure you know those supports are available to you.

Dr. Francis Christian: Well, I'm not distressed at all. Uh, it's good to be on, uh, the right side of history and to go to sleep with a good conscience. I'm thinking you guys must be really distressed because you're going against science. You're going against the WHO, and you are trying to, essentially, since you're basically doing your best to it, to censor and to silence and to muzzle intimidate, essentially physicians, scientists, and people around the world who are calling for adolescents and children not to be vaccinated. The very fact that you don't know, let me finish, because I know that you all want to jump in and cut me off. Uh, the very fact that you don't know that the WHO came out, uh, on Monday morning with the recommendation, not to vaccinate 18 and under, uh, shows that you're living in a dystopian bubble. You're only speaking to echo chambers. You don't know the level of support I have. You don't know how many surgeons, physicians, scientists in Saskatchewan, across Canada, who have reached out to me and support. You just don't know. You're living in a fantasy world of self-congratulatory messages. Uh, it's really shameful.

Dr. Susan Shaw: You see Francis, this is why we're so concerned about you because this appears to me to be a change in the way that you see the world. I've read the World Health Organization statement. I read it this morning in preparation for this meeting to make sure that, uh, I had, uh, as much information. I've read the P-hack. I've read everything. I'm very concerned about your ability to clearly see what's happening and what's happening and what others may be doing with you and to you to take advantage of your position. You are a highly intelligent man.

Dr. Francis Christian: Well, thank you.

Dr. Susan Shaw: You're not making intelligent decisions. You're interpreting literature or behaving in a way that makes me understand that you understand how to navigate a scientific debate.

Dr. Francis Christian: To be honest....

Dr. Susan Shaw: This is why it's important that we immediately reach out to the SMA health program to ensure that you have supports that you may not realize or think that you need right now, but they offer amazing support that's confidential and we will not learn about.

Dr. Francis Christian: I would recommend that you get those supports because I predict you'll be needing them very soon.

Dr. Susan Shaw: Thank you for your concern, Francis.

Male Voice 2: Thank you for that concern Francis. So, the purpose of this meeting has been accomplished, and that was to inform you of the actions taken by the College of Medicine and the SHA. I reiterate that there are mechanisms for you to appeal these decisions and a process will unfold at the university with regards to your faculty appointment. Um, again, I reiterate that the supports are available to you and that you, and they're um, excellent supports, uh, that you should consider taking advantage of. Um, but otherwise we accomplished, uh, the purpose of this meeting and you'll be getting the written documentation by email immediately

Dr. Francis Christian: Well, it wasn't really a meeting. It was basically, uh, an announcement from a, uh, a group of very, uh, deluded, uh, healthcare people. Uh, unfortunately, uh, you know, up and down the country, uh, you guys are living in a dystopian bubble. The truth will come out. And when that bubble bursts, you guys are going to be in big trouble and you think I'm in trouble. Uh, by the grace of God, I'm sleeping well at night and, uh, I'm not in any distress at all.

Male Voice 1: Well, thank you, Francis for telling us that. I'm very pleased to hear that. And again, we support, uh, if there's any services needed, we would be pleased to help and support that. Um, but the accomplishments of what was needed to be done today, uh, in terms of notification will be sent to you. And I thank you for participating in the meeting and, uh, we will get the information to you as soon as possible. Uh, as it relates to the division of general surgery, I will be discussing, uh, with the ADL, Dr. John Shaw, uh, regarding, uh, what is necessary in terms of, uh, temporary and immediate suspension of academic, uh, privileges relating to, uh, learners. Um, and as well, I'll be sending a notice, uh, as well that this is in place. So, uh, I thank you for attending the meeting and we'll end the meeting now. I appreciate your attendance. Thank you everyone.

Dr. Francis Christian: Well, thank you. Thank you.

APPENDIX 2

Dr. Peter McCullough—The Jab As The Manifest Destiny

Dr. Sam Dubé: HELLO, DR. Sam Dubé here once again for the *Toronto Business Journal* and joining me today is Dr. Peter A. McCullough, who is a clinical professor of medicine at Texas A&M college of medicine in Dallas, Texas. He's also the author and co-author of over 40 publications on COVID-19 and 600 articles in the national library of medicine. He is an internist with a subspecialty in cardiology, as well as an epidemiologist. Dr. McCullough, thank you so much for joining us here today.

Dr. Peter McCullough: Well, Dr. Dubé, it's a pleasure to be on your show and, uh, I can't say anything more fantastic regarding the efforts that you've put forward to help Canadians in the middle of this crisis.

Dr. Sam Dubé: You're very, um, kind, but, uh, I think you're the one that's really putting yourself out there and let's cut to the brass tacks right away. I saw another interview with you and I saw you on *The High Wire* with Del Bigtree with Dr. Jim Meehan. And you said all roads lead to the vaccine. Can you please elaborate?

Dr. Peter McCullough: Well, Dr. Dubé, I'll tell you the context of this as a practicing doctor, as an author, as an editor, and the president of a major medical society. Uh, people have asked me, uh, you know what authority do I have to make an opinion on this pandemic? And I have to tell you, uh, you know, I've had somebody in my family member die of this illness. I've had it myself. Um, I've had, uh, hundreds of patients fall ill with this. Um, I've advised thousands of patients nationwide. And I can tell you that this illness is treatable, that this illness can be handled by practicing doctors and practicing doctors do have the moral authority. They do have the, uh, physician authority to make the call.

What's happened here is everything has gotten out of sorts and the authority. We actually somehow, uh, are defaulting to, uh, public health agencies, uh, in the United States, we have the Centers for Disease Control, the NIH, and USFDA, they're government staffers. They actually, we pay them. They serve us. They serve doctors and patients with data with recommendations or even with products sometimes, but they in no way have authority. They in no way have moral authority. And what we're seeing with the vaccine is that it was released as the primary government answer to COVID-19, the government had no answers. They did no research or provided no strategies with respect to early treatment. It was myself and other courageous doctors that had to fill that important void.

The academic medical centres provided nothing. Do you know that, let's say at the University of Toronto, did you know that they did not seek to examine a single patient to prevent a hospitalization? They didn't set up a clinic or a tent or anything. They play defense. They just let the patients come in the hospital when they're sufficiently sick enough and to make matters worse, uh, there was a chill that was put out on any doctor attempting to treat patients with COVID-19. In fact, I get desperate messages daily from Canada. Daily. The most common question I get, Dr. Dubé, is how in the world can I get treatment for COVID-19? I do not want hospitalization. Hospitalization is a bad outcome. I'm afraid of being hospitalized and I'm afraid of dying. And so the government response has been in basically a monolithic way. The answer is it's the vaccine, all roads lead to the vaccine.

Dr. Sam Dubé: And, you know, I remember the early response of the government was like, hey, you know, you've got some symptoms, stay home, self-isolate. Only when you're really sick, present yourself to the emergency room. And you mentioned that of the 600,000 plus deaths attributed to COVID, the majority of them were due to lack of early treatment. And I mean, we can even talk about the inflation of numbers and, you know, altering, you know, death certificates and such. But the bottom line is that early treatment really is the key. And we know that many of the therapies that are used in other countries that have been approved in other countries are not here. That hydroxychloroquine, ivermectin. I interviewed Dr. Kory, his secretary told me that after his Senate address in December of 2020, I was the only person interested in interviewing him right after that Senate address. And I was stunned. I couldn't believe it. And we did an interview eight days later and you know, trying to, and, you know, the interview got shadow banned, right? So, but the therapies are out there. And you mentioned this yourself that, you know, it's a travesty that we could have gone to these people when these therapies were, were known to work, we could have administered them to people even as outpatients and prevented the vast majority of these deaths due to COVID-19.

Dr. Peter McCullough: Well, Dr. Dubé you know, the therapies work, you know, they work because if they didn't work, it wouldn't be shadow banned. It wouldn't be shadow banned, listen, if these therapies were drinking like water, you know, they'd be like a placebo, no one would care. People really care that these therapies work. They really know that they work. In fact, I was the one who set up Pierre Kory for that second set of Senate testimonies. I was the lead witness on the first set. And he showed up in his lab coat on the Senate floor in the second one and America cheered, America cheers for heroes like Pierre Kory, Paul Merrick, J. J. Roster, he testified. These are the American heroes, the hero doctors that were so courageous, they lost everything. They lost their jobs. You know, most of the early treating doctors, including myself, we got the infection ourselves. Some of us were hospitalized. One of the most courageous doctors was Vladimir Zelenko, a tiny little man who's suffering with a chronic illness. He steps out of the box when the University of Toronto and all the medical centres, the great wonderful medical centers in Canada and in the United States, when they didn't have the courage to take care of a single patient as an outpatient Vladimir Zelenko steps out of the box, in the middle of the crucible of the COVID-19 pandemic in New York. And he starts to innovate with combinations of drugs to treat COVID 19. He was enormously successful. He overcomes tremendous bias in the published literature and publishes his paper, uh, with, uh, Dr. Darwin from Germany, who helped him in the manuscript. Thank goodness. And then I was able to get a breakthrough manuscript on the concepts building upon Dr. Zelenko's work originally in *American Journal of Medicine*. And then the update was in reviews and cardiovascular medicine in December. And I'm the first author. And Zelenko the senior author. These are the stories of American heroes.

What resulted of this you're right. We lost 600,000 lives, but we were on schedule to lose 2 million. And what happened is the end of December early January, like the curves just started to get crushed. There was reduced new cases, reduced hospitalizations and deaths. The only thing that can do that is early treatment because if patients are treated at home they don't spread the illness. We shorten the duration of viral shedding from 14 days to four days, patients dramatically improve, or they certainly are able to ride it out and not be hospitalized or die. Follow-up data from, uh, Brian Proctor here in Dallas, large study, very well done, 85% reductions in hospitalizations and deaths compared to expected. And boy, we know the expected rates now.

The Cleveland Clinic even has a calculator. You can precisely calculate based on age and comorbidities, the risk of hospitalization and death. So it's not a secret. Some have said actually, Sabine Hasan, a really prominent researcher out in California, has said that we should actually not do placebo controlled trials in the middle of a pandemic. We should actually be doing other forms of study. So we don't risk people's lives and innovate with the best combinations of drugs. We knew that the virus was a fatal virus. We don't have single drugs for any fatal virus in mankind. So no single drug works for COVID-19. So the detractors to Pierre Kory said, ah ah ivermectin doesn't work. Well, course it doesn't work. No drug works alone, but drugs work in combination. And all I said is, all I need to see is a signal of benefit and acceptable safety. This is no different than HIV or Hepatitis C. No different.

All we had is those two things. We put this together in a combination, it's almost like combination chemotherapy to address viral replication, thrombosis, and cytokine, viral replication, cytokine, and thrombosis, that package. And we treat COVID-19.

We've even worked with Dr. Chatty in South Africa. He said that ivermectin and hydroxychloroquine are so politicized. He put out a tent in South Africa and he treated African, South Africans.... South Africans, Indians, waves of them treated thousands of patients. I think he had two people hospitalized. It's extraordinary. I said, how'd you do it? He goes, ivermectin. Hydroxychloroquine got so politicized I gave up on it. I timed the illness. He actually waits for certain days. And he introduces inhaled steroids, anti-inflammatories that uses anticoagulants, aspirin. And it gets them through the illness. The only way a patient in Toronto or Montreal or Vancouver ends up in the hospital is with no treatment, none. And I've looked at all the papers. If you look at the table of baseline characteristics, you ask yourself, what were they given to prevent hospitalization and death? Nothing.

Dr. Sam Dubé: No recommendations made. Now, why?

Dr. Peter McCullough: All roads lead to the vaccine. This is very important. All roads lead to the vaccine. If there was a stake, an intellectual stake put in the ground, and that stake said the way out of this crisis is going to be vaccination. That's it. Now, if somebody gets hospitalized, the doctors can do the best we can. But let me tell you, the best hospitals in America and the Stop COVID program sponsored out of Harvard. If someone requires the ICU at 28 days, the mortality is 38%. I'm telling you, hospitalization is not the answer to saving patients with COVID-19. It must be early treatment. It must be early treatment. Well, if there was an intellectual stake that said, listen, we're going to forgo early treatment. Uh, we are going to use vaccination as the major vehicle to handle this. Then we would have to prepare the public for vaccination.

We can't have the public seeking early treatment. We can't have the public being interested in nutraceuticals or in other innovations. No, let's actually try to ban all innovation. Let's suppress it. Let's keep people in lockdown in fear. Let's keep complete control over this, and then drive this intellectual stake for mass vaccination.

I published an op-ed in The Hill, appears to a series of last year. I was a regular contributor for the first time in a political journal of interests, but I needed a window to America published one last summer. And I said the great gamble of the COVID-19 vaccine, um, uh, solution and the reason why it was such a gamble, because it was a huge stake. It was obvious governments work and invest in early inventory treatment. Canada's done nothing in terms of large multi-drug trials. Neither have we in the United States. I'm a cardiologist, Dr. Dubé. We do trials of 20,000 patients routinely to reduce risks of mal cardio infarction and death, or reduced hospitalization and death and heart failure.

Suddenly in COVID where we're swamped with patients, we have budgets that are flushed with cash, and we can't execute on a single trial. Do you know the national institutes of health, had a meagre trial where they were going to use hydroxychloroquine and azithromycin. I mean, that's like the most basic thing. Vladimir Zelenko was doing that back in March. They put together the most meagre trial, 2000 patients at Stanford and other centers all lined-up. They hired the nurses, they distributed the drugs, they had the binders, they had everything all set and then inexplicably, they said, you know, we're going to close down after 20 patients, people like, what, was there a problem? What happened with the 20 patients? They said, oh no, the hydroxychloroquine was fine. There wasn't any safety problems. It's like, how can you just, I mean, that is just, we just don't invest in research like that, spend all that money and then just give up. I mean, we were swimming with patients. We were swimming the patients.

So what we did is through the summer, I basically decided, uh, things are derailed here. We're not getting any of our publications in. Our governments are not investing anything in early treatment. In fact, they're suppressing early treatment. We said, you know what? We're taking this to the people. And thankfully we have the Association of American Physicians and Surgeons. They're kind of the hero organization they had at early on sued the American government saying, why'd you buy all the hydroxychloroquine and hog it into a stockpile? Get that distributed. What's all that about? That's going to make it even harder to use hydroxychloroquine.

They actually sued the government. I said, wow, I like that organization. I wasn't a member, but that took some chutzpah. I ended up joining them and we joined forces and we published the, uh, the first, uh, COVID 19 home treatment guide, which is enormously successful, was published in October. It has been downloaded, I think over a million times in the first run, probably tens of millions of times. And when I say early treatment kicked in, they kicked in because we had the home treatment guide, which had already organized things. We now have four national telemedicine services,15 regional telemedicines, 250 treating doctors in United States. We have mail-order pharmacies. Even when the pharmacies want to decline patients' drugs, we use mail-order pharmacies. We get the drugs to the patient's house the next day. We basically have taken over health care.

I don't even think our government agencies know. They don't even know that there is a network of hero doctors that is basically taken over and you know what? We're not alone. There's Panda started in South Africa. They're not worldwide. We have the Burton Heart Group in the UK. We've got Treatment Domiciliari in Italy. They just have taken over. They're just treating Italians at home. And then we have a COVID Medical Research Network in Australia. So we've got a great team. And this is a story about courage. It's a story about heroes. And it's a story about stakeholders who I think have basically worked, whether it's together or separately, but for a common set of processes. And they are to create as much fear, suffering, hospitalization and death in order to promote mass vaccination.

Dr. Sam Dubé: So stakeholders, you're talking about the NIH, you're talking about the CDC, you're talking about the FDA. You're talking about big pharma, essentially. The people that hold all the patents to the vaccines and the average person may not even know that there's a vested financial interest in promoting these vaccines. And it can be just as simple as that. Is that they're promoting the vaccines, suppressing the early therapy, the early treatments in order to get the dream of a needle in every arm, which is a nightmare. Ultimately, I mean, there are studies coming out now showing that people who've had COVID-19 actually have a much higher incidence of adverse effects if they get vaccinated. Isn't that correct?

Dr. Peter McCullough: That's right. I mean, if you wanted a needle in every arm I'd say, listen, make a safer vaccine. I mean, this is crazy. It's like, oh, I want a needle in every arm, vaccine is good for you. It's like, well, make a safe one. Why don't you just make a saline placebo. I'd sign up for that. Just make people happy. Sure. I'll take a sailing shot. Good. I did it fine.

Dr. Sam Dubé: You are not anti-vaxx, you are pro-vaccine, you're pro pretty much any vaccine.

Dr. Peter McCullough: I mean, good grief. You know, 98% of Americans take all the vaccines. I've had two vaccines this year. I've had the flu vaccine and the shingles vaccine because I'm of the age that I'm supposed to have it. So come on. I've had every single vaccine I'm supposed to have, but when the COVID-19 vaccine got rolled out, it was studied in pretty limited populations, you know, healthy people. The J and J program had 60% with no medical problems. I can tell you as an internist and cardiologist, I saw a ton of patients yesterday at the hospital. Everybody has medical problems. I don't have people with no medical problems, my patients are getting vaccinated. You know, a lot of them wouldn't even be in these trials, but specifically they excluded pregnant women, women of childbearing potential. COVID recovered, suspected COVID recovered children. They were all out.

And I tell you what, when you exclude patients from studies in the investigational review board applications, there must be a justification for it. And I can tell you the justification for excluding those groups is that they had no opportunity for benefit. And they had expected harm, very importantly, expected harm. So when we have a situation like this, and then the vaccines get rolled out, if it was doctors controlling the vaccine program, the last thing we do is vaccinate these groups because they weren't studied. That's like a golden rule. Doctors don't do this, but instead the program has rolled out doctors not involved. Where's the moral authority of the doctor here? No, these are rolled out, there are vaccine centres. Doctors are not even involved, there are volunteers. And then the vaccine centres basically say, we're open, come on in and let us vaccinate you. And so, you know, which was really sadly pregnant women

Dr. Sam Dubé: First pregnant woman, they didn't even test on pregnant women and, you know, phase three, there you go. Volunteer. We'll take volunteers of pregnant women, right?

Dr. Peter McCullough: And they started vaccinating pregnant women. And the horrors just start to play out over time. When the vaccines came out of the clinical trials program, because they had exclusion criteria and they had data safety monitoring boards, clinical event committees, uh, institutional review boards, their vaccines in the trials were reasonably safe. I mean, they caused 80% of people had reactions in the arm, but when they came out they were safe. What doctor in the world would not just follow those clinical trials and recommend the vaccine, which is what I did. About 70% of my patients got the vaccine in December, January, February. It was over with. Pretty much got everybody vaccinated. That was great. But then what happened? That just wasn't enough. The vaccine stakeholders said, you know, come on, we got to do more. And a needle in every arm. And people were saying, wait a minute. You know, young people don't need it. They, get COVID, but the natural immunity is better anyway. Uh, why take a risk of a vaccine?

And then it just kept going and going. And so the statements now that we're seeing, uh, for instance, there's some from our regulatory agencies, our CDC, if you were to go on Twitter and type in COVID-19 vaccine in pregnancy, there'll be a video from our CDC with one of the staffers. And what she says is they say, we have no reason not to believe that it's safe. Right? So it was kind of like, oh you're not going to catch me on this one. Um, and of course, and so here we have a giant investigation. There's no clinical event committee. There's no data safety monitoring board. There's no ethics committee and there are no methods in place for risk mitigation. Risk mitigation is important. You know, I have chaired several dozen data safety monitoring boards. I've been the overall principal investigator of worldwide studies. I've worked very carefully with the FDA. We always have risk mitigation. And what the public should know is that doctors and researchers, we have a method to reduce the risk of anything we try in an investigation. And what we needed to see is, and we still need to see, we need to see methods to reduce death and hospitalization after vaccination. And, uh, the other side is said, oh, but they're not due to the vaccine. Is that it doesn't matter. The FDA doesn't matter.

Dr. Sam Dubé: I know, I mean you mentioned it, like we've got over 4,000 deaths reported on the VAERS site, which has problems. And you detail some of those problems with not being able to input the second dosing and not being able to input people who've recovered from COVID. So you have no record of that, and then over 12,000 hospitalizations. And, yet, um, with this problem, we're only getting maybe between 1 and 10% of, of these adverse reactions and death reporting. I'm talking to colleagues, I'm talking to people finding out that, well, it's really hard to report, or, you know, my doctor said not to report, it can't be due to the vaccine. And you even mentioned that the initial 1600 some deaths, they kind of hand waved and said, no, we determined that all those cases are not due to the vaccine. Meanwhile, there are videos circulating of people minutes after getting vaccinated, uh, going into convulsions and dying. And you're saying that's not due to the vaccine. Really, really. Wow. Just, wow.

Dr. Peter McCullough: Well, Dr. Dubé, it gets worse. Just a few days ago, the CDC doubled down and they said, you know, we're at 4,800 deaths and we still don't think any are related to the vaccine again, but not having an external clinical event committee, a day safety monitoring committee, how in the world? One of their first statements was that the CDC and FDA doctors of which, by the way, there are very few practicing doctors, and I don't think any expert in clinical trials, they reviewed the cases and they didn't think any were related to the vaccine. Well, that's like, you know, that's like asking what if they ask Pfizer if Pfizer thinks, but of course those people are biased. They're stakeholders. They have a stake in the execution of the program. In fact, the national institutes of health co-owns the packet patent with Moderna. The NIH is no different than Moderna.

I mean, this is the type of thing where the conflict of interest is so extraordinary. We have to break this wide open and have external experts get into this. So, and that's happened. So the VAER system you're right, is flawed because it underreports. We know now that 83% of the entries in the VAER system, including some I've done, are done by doctors and healthcare workers who are concerned. I had to take time at the end of the day. It took me half an hour to do this and fill out all the forms. And I couldn't do it completely because I couldn't figure out how to get all the data in there. But I had to. The poor woman was hospitalized with blood clots all over. It was awful. It was after I think Pfizer, Moderna, and I was entering all this information in and at the bottom of each form. It said warning, um, punishable by federal fines or imprisonment. Believe me, if the CDC says 4,800, it could be 48,000 people. We know in the 4800, 40% of them die on days one, two, and three. So Dr. Dubé, as a doctor, who's seen a lot of patients who are healthy enough to go out to a vaccine centre, what is the chances that there's going to be a big blip like that on days one, two, and three?

Dr. Sam Dubé: Slim and none, you know? And they're hand-waving that away. It's unbelievable. It's unconscionable. And you know, when we talk about conflict of interest, you look at other domains, for instance, athletics. You don't get the coach to be a judge for their athlete. Do you know what I mean? There are so many other domains, even the financial world. You can't have these kind of overt conflicts of interest. And yet here they do. How does that happen? And how does it get by the public? You know what I mean? When you got the CDC having dozens of active vaccines, and this was known, this was even publicized over a year ago, various documentaries, things, these things were verifiable. They weren't even denied by these governing bodies by these public health bodies. And yet what's going on now is this systematic kind of campaign. And like you said, either working together or alone or not, but with maybe a similar kind of agenda, um, in order to misinform people in order to instill fear in people, um, in order to get a needle in every arm. And, you know, you mentioned yourself, it really, the vaccine should be contraindicated in a good chunk of the population because they've been exposed to COVID-19 and the research is now coming out, that it's dangerous for them, more dangerous.

And just recently here in Canada, and I know you have a vested interest because your wife is Canadian and your wife's parents are in Toronto. And, you know, the kind of lockdowns that we're going through right now. And it being now June of

2021. And we're hopefully at the end of the stay at home order, even the police. The majority of the police force have said, we're not going to enforce these new draconian laws. And our premier had to tearfully withdraw the, you know, the new powers he had allegedly given the police to stop people randomly and find them and arrest them.

Uh, if they weren't deemed to be essential or have any business being outside, it's 25 degrees celsius out there right now. And people are, they're not heeding the stay-at-home order. They are keeping within their bubbles, you know, to an extent. We need to educate people anyway, I'm rambling, but I'm just saying that there's so much going on out there, Dr. McCullough, that is misinformation or hiding things on the Canadian government site. They just said, and I screenshotted it this morning that, um, for vaccines, you're better off getting the vaccine and experiencing potential side effects, than getting the actual virus, because they were trying to address the idea of natural immunity versus vaccine immunity. And in medical school, they taught us in general, natural immunity is far superior and more broad-spectrum and longer lasting than vaccine immunity.

That's medicine 101. You know what I mean? We all know that because the mechanisms are different and there's different types of immunity, you know, the innate versus the adaptive and humoral versus the cellular. But then they say this on the site, it's like, no, that's totally not true for COVID-19. Even by the CDC own statistics. It's totally not true. A good chunk of the population is not in major danger of severe, um, adverse symptoms and death. And yet they're saying this in their comparing it to meningitis on that site, they're comparing it to not being vaccinated versus meningitis. It's like, how can you make that comparison?

Dr. Peter McCullough: Let me just respond to that by saying that, um, we know by good work by actually Dr. Brown in Canada, uh, the clinical trials in the vaccine program, during the heat of the pandemic, we had really high rates of COVID back then, that whether a patient got placebo or they got the vaccine, there was less than a 1% chance they would get COVID over two months, actually three months of being in the program, less than 1%. So I'm telling you it doesn't. We could be injecting saline in these vaccines centres. These people are going to have a less than 1% chance of getting COVID. The average person getting a vaccine, they think that they're walking into shopping malls and they're getting bombarded with COVID. They are not, they, if we would inject them with nothing, they would have less than a 1% chance of getting COVID.

The vaccine program is going to be successful, and it's going to look like it's successful because the pandemic is going to burn itself out. I mean, this is ridiculous that I've already said, I've already told America on national TV. I said, listen, don't attribute any change in these epidemic curves to vaccination. It's mathematically impossible. Dr. Brown said that.

Dr. Sam Dubé: I'm a mathematician. And I will tell you.

Dr. Peter McCullough: It's not gonna happen. So this idea of, well, if you get COVID, you're better off taking all this risk with the vaccine, as opposed to risking COVID. Uh, Andy Boston, who's former epidemiologists from Framingham, we've been working carefully with him. We think that argument may play out when you get over age 50, or with some medical problems. Some people say over 65 is probably a very narrow band of people who are healthy enough to withstand the vaccine, but at high enough risk with COVID because maybe they're a bus driver or a barber, or a healthcare worker, fine, uh, nursing home workers, a hundred percent because they gave the seniors, um, COVID and, uh, they gave it to them, you know, nursing home workers should have been ground zero for vaccination. That was awful what happened, ground zero.

And then outside of that, I had estimated maybe 20 million, maybe 20 million Americans. That's it. And if we limit it to 20 million, we would have limited the chances of an explosion of safety events, But no, those who want a needle in every arm wouldn't listen to that. They want everybody. And it's interesting who they really want. They've kind of given up on seniors. You don't hear anything on the advertisement about seniors getting vaccinated. It's almost, that's actually, it's been interesting. It's almost been absent in their public messaging. The public is, the messaging is we want the kids. We want kids and pregnant women.

Dr. Sam Dubé: So let's address that. I just want to go back to this full effectiveness thing. So this is where the whole 95% effectiveness of the vaccine comes in, mixing-up absolute risk with relative risk. And you were talking about a less than 1% chance of getting COVID. And I remember one of the studies of 27,000 people, they were talking about 0.8% of the population and that getting reduced to 0.04. So the absolute, the risk was reduced by 0.76%. Just like you said, it was under 1% for the vaccine, getting the vaccine. They have to vaccinate 132 people, according to Dr. Jim Neon's presentation, in order to prevent one case of COVID. And yet these 132, 133 people have to subject themselves to potential adverse effects. And imagine if they were exposed to COVID-19 or had it, which the CDC admits cause 6 to 24 times, uh, the number of cases of COVID. So there's a huge number of people out there who may have been exposed, who were at risk of a needle in every arm, right? Like it's just, it's unconscionable.

Dr. Peter McCullough: Well, actually, that's a great analysis, that in that situation, there's zero chance they can benefit. So if a rare thing happened with the vaccine and you vaccinated enough of those people without benefit, all you're going to do is stack up safety events with no benefit. I testified in the Texas Senate, March 10th of this year, of 2021, uh, by CDC standard equations, uh, that we are at 80% herd immunity. And people say, well, gosh, you know, it doesn't really jive with what we think. I said, that doesn't mean it's over with. It just means it can't spread that far. And I think it was a few days after that, they had a Texas Rangers game, they had a full stadium, I don't know, of 60,000 people in the stadium. And we have very good public health down here. If there was an outbreak, it would have been captured, believe me.

And in fact, they were looking at that. They wanted to find it, nothing. And then one of the public health officials backed me up a few weeks later and said, you know, Dr. McCullough is right. We're at 80% herd immunity. Texas, we never locked down. Never, you know, we took some more conservative measures. We always, uh, I live right here in Dallas. I'm going to go out to restaurants tonight. We've opened restaurants the entire time. We had a big early treatment state. We had a lot of these independent doctors that just treated it. And, um, uh, we would never overflowed our hospitals. And we ended up about 24 in the United States in terms of cases, per million and deaths per million population. And we have a massive Hispanic population and a massive immigrant population. And they live in multi-generational households without a lot of good documentation.

So I got to tell you in Texas, if we can do it. Look what Florida did. Florida never locked down. They just went all the way through. They had tons of seniors. If there's going to be a place where there's going to be mortality. Do you know how many Canadians go down to Florida for, it's unbelievable. It would have been like wildfire, the fact that we have such a different pandemic response, even within an East State in the United States that tells you something. Anytime there's variation in what people are doing, that means, ooh, something's off here.

Dr. Sam Dubé: Exactly. Well, I mean, the states are empowered to have a little bit more of an independent response. Up here in Canada our, uh, minority government, and the official opposition are completely in agreement over these lockdowns. And, uh, and also, uh, ignoring questions about, uh, other therapies. So for instance, the Manitoba premier was questioned by a reporter. I don't know how that question got through, but it did, uh, about ivermectin. And he completely ignored the question and answered it with some, you know, stock statement about trying to produce vaccines in Canada, thanked everyone and took off. And it was like, you gotta be kidding me. That was so blatant. It was so blatant. And I really appreciate you, uh, Dr. McCollough addressing some, uh, Canada specific issues here, but, you know we're all in this together, ultimately, and I want to bring it back to, you were talking about pregnant women and children.

And you mentioned how I can't recall which state it was, was it North Carolina, where they were. And so children under 12 being told, Hey, you can get the vaccine without parental consent. You're old enough to make the decision. It's happening here in Toronto. Uh, and I have the PDF where they actually declare it. We have the legislation for this allegedly where children can just go. Yeah. Yeah. I made the decision. I want the vaccine. They give you ice cream, give you the vaccine. And you told me you've seen video of, um, um, um, adults being cordoned-off and children going in and in the vaccine, what is up with that and moral authority? You tell me.

Dr. Peter McCullough: Well, I think, uh, Canadians and Americans listening to this, ought to ask themselves, are things being done now that break all the rules, that break all the norms? And if they are, who's breaking the rules? Is it Dr. McCullough? Is it Dr. Dubé? What rule have I broken, you know? I take care of patients every day. I have a bunch of prescriptions I have to refill as soon as I get off of this. I can tell you, I am not breaking a single law. If someone gets sick and I treat them with ivermectin, hydroxychloroquine, and I give them some prednisone or Lovenox or aspirin, I am not breaking any law. Why uh, is our authorities now breaking conventions, and some of these things are written in law. We have an Office of Human Research Protections, OHRP they have been silent. They have what's called a legally authorized representative. An individual under age 18 in the office of human research subject protection must have a LAR, a legally authorized representative.

That means a parent. You have to have a parent sign. You must do that. So when a state in the setting of an investigation, and that it is an investigation, it says right in the form, you are participating in an investigation. You must have a legally authorized representative. The fact that a state is going to do this now and say, you know what? I'm going to break human protections law. I'm going to break the law. And we are going to in a sense lure kids into school and pressure and coerce them to take the vaccine or lure them from an ice cream and keep them away from their parents. You know, what's going to stop this, is Canadians and Americans waking up out of a trance. They are in a trance. They are brainwashed. They are actually, oh, yes. Here take my child and vaccinate them. There have been, I was on, um, Dan Ball Real News two days ago with an outbreak of myocarditis.

This vaccine is taken, and it was circulating spike protein, which is dangerous, circulates for two weeks. We've never used this technology. Now talk about experimental. This technology is science fiction. This Wuhan spike protein, which is the product of bioterrorism research. That's not what we are allowing in people's bodies.

Dr. Sam Dubé: And that's starting to come out now, in the Fauci emails, just came out a few days ago, right? The redacted parts are the parts we really want to know about, right?

Dr. Peter McCullough: This is bioterrorism by injection, basically. And what's happening is the Wuhan spike protein. Your body is tricked into producing enough for two weeks, as little kids are producing tremendous amounts of Wuhan spike protein. Remember with COVID-19. It comes in through the respiratory tract and the kids can just fight it down. They've got a thymus, they just knock it down. COVID is nothing for them, but you let them, you give them a main line of this stuff and you don't let the kids normal defences, defend against it. This spike protein eats them up. So it causes a tremendous, uh, uh, chest pain elevations in cardiac troponin, heart damage, EKG changes. There was a rash in California two days ago. There were 18 cases. Last night in Connecticut, the families are scrambling. We've already seen kids with blood clotting events, uh, thrombosis in the brain, young athlete.

I mean, these are tragic situations that children have no opportunity for benefit. Only an opportunity for harm. Well, listen to this regulatory malfeasance. Now Pfizer went to the FDA on May 10th and said, well, we're done with our age 12 to 15 trial, give us approval. And with no data, no safety data. What happened was the FDA looked at it and said, well, the antibodies went up. Uh, we think it's generally safe here. You're approved. We never do that. Never, never, never. There should have been incredible scrutiny on safety. Nothing. That's on May 10th. So it's approved based on antibody response, May 10th. The FDA separate division on May 19th says don't measure antibodies. Nope. They're not indicative of immunity, but the FDA puts that out there as a statement in order to try to dissuade people from uncovering their immunity and not taking the vaccine. Wait a minute. They approve it on May 10th. And then suddenly the antibodies don't imply immunity then, and then on May 27th, the data come out in the *New England Journal of Medicine*. 2300 kids vaccinated, aged 12 to 15.

Parents need to listen to this. 2300 kids vaccinated. Two-to-one, uh, active versus placebo randomization. The entire program prevented 18 cases of the sniffles. I mean, the kids with COVID-19 get just about nothing. 18 cases, that's it. And 60 to 80% of the kids on shot one or shot two got really sick. We're talking fevers of 38, 39 and 40, muscle aches, body aches, joint aches, nausea, vomiting… want to give them Tylenol. Kids in 30 or 40% of cases need Tylenol. These kids go to school, you know, my conclusion for me in that paper and the *New England Journal or Medicine*, and I just published a paper in the *New England Journal of Medicine* this month.

So let me tell you, I know what I'm talking about. My interpretation of that paper would be don't vaccinate children. That's my interpretation. I'm telling Canada and America, that's my interpretation, as a doctor with authority. I'm telling you don't vaccinate children. That's my interpretation. The interpretation of the authors: vaccinate them. The termination of the FDA, CDC: vaccinate them. Canadian authorities, people are in a trance and these poor children have got nowhere to go, if the parents can't protect the children, if we cannot do that, that is a fundamental responsibility, no matter what government, no matter what country, no matter if we're being bombed overhead or we're drowned in a flood. No matter what, as parents, if we cannot protect our children, that family circle is crushed and we're crushed as a society.

Dr. Sam Dubé: You know, Dr. McCullough, there are so many things I want to talk to you about and ask you. But there is one thing that I want to say. And, um, you were speaking on the high wire and saying that, you know, you come from a place of moral authority, as a physician, as a clinical physician, you have so much more experience than, uh, the bureaucrats and, uh, the MDs that, you know, much like some of our officials here, um, are just, you know, seem to be following some kind of script or you know, like financial, uh, plan or something like this, or avoiding personal harm or personal financial harm. Um, you said, bring it on. You said, bring it on, bring on the censorship, bring on. And I have to say, I'm scared. Like I'm scared, like legitimately scared because the level of, let's use the word misinformation, and misleading is profound. And it's the highest level. And, you know, here we are discussing this as free people, um, you as a clinical physician and me as an academic physician and trying to educate people, and you're doing God's work by the way, I have to say. And my hats off to you, many hats, you know.

But it looks like there's something happening at every turn and the wheels of progress in the areas of freedom of speech and personal liberty, and the ability to make decisions about one's health are turning so slowly. And if you look at how many people needlessly died because they couldn't get the early treatment, how many children are going to be potentially affected for life? How many pregnant women, 275 at last count up until near the end of May miscarrying, with that number potentially being grossly under-reported and maybe over 2000, right? According to the statistics on reporting. How many more people are going to have to suffer, Dr. McCullough?

Dr. Peter McCullough: Well, especially with pregnant women, which we can treat anyway, you know, we give, uh, if a woman had systemic lupus and a high fever, or really active rheumatoid arthritis, we treat her with hydroxychloroquine anyway. Preeclampsia, we treat with aspirin anyway. I just had a patient yesterday in clinic, and she had been treated with Lovenox through her pregnancy because she had a deep venous thrombosis. So listen, we can use drugs in pregnancy and we can get pregnant women through the illness. I mentioned in my family, we actually had a death and it was a young pregnant woman, and it was tragic. And so on my wife's side, because it was early in March and we didn't know what was going on. And actually when she died, she still didn't have a diagnosis of COVID because we didn't have the tests. We look at all the patterns. It's for sure she had it.

She was probably one of the few maternal deaths at a major medical center in the last five years. So it's not a common thing. And so we put it together. We believe it's COVID, but that was early on. We know a lot right now we know a lot. And the bottom line is we can treat COVID during pregnancy. Uh, vaccinating patients during pregnancy is dangerous. It's irresponsible, it's reckless, they haven't been sufficiently studied. There was a woman in my church. Uh, uh, she had the advice of an obstetrician and, uh, she got vaccinated at six months and two days later, no baby heartbeat. And she has to go in and have a stillbirth. You know, doctors are complicit in this. I've always said, I think a part of this is the fear of the lack that we're not meeting anymore. And I think if we brought a hundred prominent obstetricians into a room and we sat down and went over the data about COVID-19 in pregnancy, what the risks are, how we can treat it.

And then we present the vaccine, the messenger RNA "vaccines." We present to obstetricians that the vaccine makes the body produce for two weeks at high concentrations, a product of bio-terrorism. The Wuhan spike protein that's been genetically altered to be lethal. Okay. And we review the data. We review the abortions and miscarriages reported out of Canada and the United States. And then we sat down, we had a round table discussion. I don't think a hundred obstetricians will walk out of that room saying, yeah, we should vaccinate the pregnant women. I think right now doctors are in a trance or they're kind of brainwashed, they're in fear. They're like, uh, yeah my society says that they should be vaccinated, they should be vaccinated. These poor women are like, doctor, really should I? So what's going to happen is we take the message to the people. Um, uh, our vaccine centres, um, uh, have really started to empty out in the United States, starting April 8th. We have the data. I go by the vaccine center every single day, and it's empty.

They have police officers out to direct traffic. They've got cones, they got a huge parking lot, no takers. Uh, we have about half of Americans have been vaccinated. And what we're starting to see for the first time was we're starting to see some remorse.

We're starting to see some regretfulness, clearly, of the thousands and thousands of people that injured with the vaccine. They are clearly more civil, some are angry and they are writing about it, but then we have others who have gotten the vaccine and then they think about it and they start to see the horrific data out. Um, you know, our chief of surgery contacted me recently about a dramatic case of a huge blood clot that clogged off a heart valve and it shouldn't have happened.

And then he texted me back recently. He says, you know, uh, how's it going with the vaccine? And he's a surgeon. He's not following this. I just sent him the scoreboard from the VAERS system for the vaccine complications. You know, we're up to, in the middle of May 4,400 plus hospitals, uh, of deaths. 14,000 hospitalizations what have you? And I sent it to him, because well are these big numbers or not? I said, listen, the scoreboard ought to be less than 200 for every vaccine. There are vaccines we use more than COVID. Flu is one.

Dr. Sam Dubé: I mean look at the swine flu vaccine in 1976. How many millions of people got vaccine? What, 45 million? And how many deaths did it take for them to stop completely and realized, whoops, we made a mistake. It was what, 25?

Dr. Peter McCullough: 25 deaths and 55 million vaccinations, 500 cases. Again .. to stop it. And here we are in the United States today, let's say we have 160 million people vaccinated. And the scary thing is what's in the VAERS has permanent VAERS numbers. That means the CDC has confirmed. They indeed died. They indeed hospitalized. There are probably a mountain of temporary VAERs that's going to be converted to permanent. And what we're hearing from inside sources, is that what we're seeing is just January. Can you imagine once we get to February, March and April, these numbers are going to skyrocket, and I think it's even possible, the vaccine stakeholders are delaying on getting the safety numbers, uh, into this, uh, public viewing in order to promote more vaccination. At some point in time, America has to be scared off. I think they're already scared of about half the people have been vaccinated. Many are regretful, and the people who are left are just saying, you know, listen, I've seen enough. My uncle died with this. My aunt was hospitalized. Everybody knows somebody in their circle now injured with the vaccine.

So, uh, you know, like I said, 70% of my patients vaccinated. December, January, February, I'm looking at the data now. I'm looking at the behavior of the CDC and FDA and NIH and it's looking less and less trustable every day, honestly. So I do not, uh, recommend, as a blanket recommendation the vaccine for my patients. If I had a new patient tomorrow and based on risks and benefits, I may recommend the vaccine using my clinical judgment, my moral authority, if you will, but it's not a general, um, uh, recommendation. Now, yesterday I was on Hugh Hewitt radio show, and it was hundreds of people called in, uh, because I thought he was, it was a real hatchet job. He's a real pro vaccer. And he was gonna really take me down and discredit me, I use the word discredit a bunch of times with like, as if that's what he was trying to do. But we did get to the discussion of moral authority.

He said, Dr. McCullough, what do you think about this? If somebody listens to you today and they don't take the vaccine and they get COVID and they die, don't you feel like you have a moral responsibility for that death?

And I said, you know, I, I said, you know, whether they take the vaccine or they don't to take the vaccine, I treat them the same way. I said, they get COVID anyway. You know, because people are thinking like the vaccine is absolute, it will prevent COVID. And the only way to get COVID is to not take the vaccine.

It's not true. As a matter of fact there were 10,000, uh, break-through, really well documented breakthrough infections that the CDC logged up until the end of um, of, uh, April, uh, uh, end of May I'm sorry and they gave up. They gave up and we have no idea how many they looked at. We have no idea. We don't know if they took a random sample or what. They had 10,000. I mean, it's hard, they have to do phone calls. You've got to figure out if somebody had COVID or not. I bet that's 10 X underestimate. I bet there's hundred thousand or more breakthrough cases.

There's already been projections in the UK because so many people are vaccinated. They're still having COVID. So the bottom line is they're predicting 60 to 70% of their COVID is going to be vaccinated.

So how can you create a "vaccine passport" when you get COVID anyway? How can you make this? What are you going to do with a vaccine passport? Are you going to sit on your privileged, uh, uh, train ride, and just cough on each other and give each other COVID? And the interesting thing is that COVID-re-covered. Those are the people you really care about. Cause they can't get COVID. They can't receive it. They're perfectly immune. I mean uh, last year I watched the Stanley Cup playoffs, and now I got the Canadians attention and you know what the Dallas stars were in it. And the Dallas Stars, they kind of ran out of gas, uh, Dr. Dubé at the end, but, um, you know, they were in it and it was up, I think it was mainly in, um, uh, in, uh, Calgary or Edmonton. But the bottom line is they had this, they put a big cover over all the seats.

It was just a big sea of gray.

Well, you know what they could have done. They could have invited a bunch of American and Canadian COVID recovered patients. They could have come into town. They could have had a lot of that um, Labatt's beer and had hot dogs. And they could have went to hockey games all the time, huge amount of revenue. And nobody would have gotten a single case of COVID. If we could have recognized that

COVID-recovered is the golden immunity. But to this day, I'm, COVID recovered. I go in the hospital every day, wearing a mask. Um, you know, I do anything, wear a mask. I'm trying to take a trip, uh, my first vacation in over a year to Hawaii next week. And guess what? I've got to go to Walgreens because I have to get a COVID test. Why? I've already had it.

And so this inability to recognize COVID-recovered has been over with. At some point in time, I got to say, listen, it's over with, it's almost as if the stakeholders want this misery to go on. They never want it to be over with, you know, because they've already told us, listen, if you finally capitulate and you take the vaccine, which is what everybody wants you to do, take the vaccine. Guess what?

Dr. Sam Dubé: Everything goes back to normal.

Dr. Peter McCullough: No. Within a few months, it's not over.

Dr. Sam Dubé: No, you got variants too.

Dr. Peter McCullough: Yeah. Now you got the booster. Now you've got the booster. So it's not over with. So if you finally get your passport, you can't get it renewed until you get the booster. If you've got your hospital staff privileges, you can't get a booster. So something is going on here. This is the gift that keeps giving. And part of this is not recognizing COVID recovered. Something about. So there is a demand letter in to the CDC with all the data. It's 200 pages long, legal letter, saying listen, you must recognize COVID recovered. Every time you put vaccine here in your recommendations, recommend COVID recovery. If vaccinated patients can go do something in a shopping mall, well so can COVID-recovered.

Dr. Sam Dubé: Right...

Dr. Peter McCullough: But it's better immunity.

Dr. Sam Dubé: Absolutely, and you even recommended the T detect test, which looks for small changes in the chromosomes of the T-cells of an individual in their tissue sample, uh, that basically shows that they've got permanent immunity, uh, from COVID-19. And, uh, so, you know, we should mention that website later on in the commentary, but what I'm really afraid of Dr. McCullough is this idea of antibody-dependent enhancement. And I'm afraid that mass vaccination, especially people who've had COVID-19, may in fact either produce more variants or make them worse for people, um, to say in layman's terms and what do you say to that?

Dr. Peter McCullough: Well, I just did a program in part with, um, with Asia Pacific and Mike Ryan for the Australians, New Zealand and all those in the Asia Pacific on that, based on a paper that actually came out of Australia on antibody-dependent enhancement, and Ray Skewy, who's been a co-author with me on several publications has been on Fox News, as early as last spring for the United States saying, wait a minute, if we vaccinate people, and because the spike protein is not the whole virus, we're going to get a pretty narrow library of antibodies. And if we're not careful, the antibodies can configure a certain way. And instead of neutralizing the virus, they can actually invite more viral particles in. And lo and behold, we have seen this in my view in just one application and it came in the Pfizer submission to the FDA briefing booklet. Actually the best sources of information honestly about the vaccines are the regulatory documents, and they're available online. They're really good. In the FDA briefing. Um, I want to say actually on page 42, I'll tell your readers to go there, page 42. Interestingly, after the first shot of messenger RNA, there's actually increased risk of COVID-19 with the vaccine compared to placebo. It makes no sense.

And then sure enough, they described that out of Israel and they showed our friends. Now after the second shot, things settled down. So it's either the circulating spike protein that kind of beats up the cells. And then if you are exposed, the virus comes in or is the early immature library of antibodies that are not yet sterilizing, that they actually enhance the risk of disease. That's antibody-dependent enhancement. What many virologists are thinking about long-term are two issues. Let's say in the United States we have 120 million people vaccinated. And let's just say, all of them were previously unexposed, which isn't true. But if they were, that means we have 120 million people who have the narrowest immunity in the world. It is a narrow strip. There are maybe just 50 antibodies to the spike protein. Do you know the natural infection creates thousands and thousands.

Dr. Sam Dubé: 1400... right?

Dr. Peter McCullough: Yeah of cellular changes. I mean the natural immunity is so robust you're not going to get COVID again. That's it you're done. But obviously the CDC in a really short period of time had a ton of cases. They had thousands of cases. So we know this narrow library of antibodies is not good enough. The viral particles can scoop by. Well if the virus configures in a certain way, the antibodies may actually help an infection long-term. That's big time antibody enhancement. That'd be like, wow. If someone figured out the antibodies to the spike protein, which is bio-terrorism, the same people working on the bio-terrorism configure out another weapon to actually, um, enable antibody-dependent enhancement as a bioterrorist weapon that's possible, or the other possibility is just create such a strong mutant, like we're seeing this in India, the double mutant that just blew past the, uh, the vaccine. So anyway, you cut the mustard very narrow immunity based on the spike protein is a disaster, you know, even in, even in influenza, we have four or five different epitopes. In pneumococcal vaccine, we've got like 23 now. I mean, the COVID-19 vaccine is very, very limited rush technology.

Dr. Sam Dubé: Yeah. I mean that spike, the original spike protein is not in its, you know, not that same form anymore, right? Like we're giving vaccines to people that potentially may not be sensitive to that original spike protein, right?

Dr. Peter McCullough: Right, right. So there's so much, we don't know. Um, uh, the Wuhan spike protein, the wild type that's gone now. The CDC keeps track of variants. We got 14 new variants, most common one United States is a UK variant, but also it is known. It is known. It came out in one of the emails released, uh, yesterday. It's known that not only the gain of function, uh, research, uh, in changing the spike protein at the fear and... showing. But it's also known that there are four loops of RNA that are inserted there that belong to the HIV virus. So in the spike protein, there's some, you get some bonus HIV in it. Terrific. So whether you've had the natural infection, which I did, I'm not thrilled about it, but I've had some HIV RNA in my body, or whether you take the vaccine and you intentionally put it in your body, you are getting some HIV RNA. And when those epitopes were exposed early in one of the Australian vaccines.

Dr. Sam Dubé: They tested positive for HIV.

Dr. Peter McCullough: A hundred percent. Can you imagine being a young person, you sign up for a vaccine trial and you get the gift of now having a positive HIV test without actually having HIV. And you got to explain that on the dating apps, you know, they're talking about using. In United States, they had on the news that it's going to be on a dating app that you took the COVID-19 vaccine. I'm not sure that's such a good idea. In fact, one of the comedians said, why don't they have, um, the status on chlamydia, gonorrhea, and herpes? That'd be more informative. This COVID-19 vaccine for young people is probably a setback.

Dr. Sam Dubé: Yeah. It's not one of the dating apps, it's apparently a whole bunch of the dating apps. And, you know I for one would be like, okay, thanks for announcing that to me actually. I'd like to know who got vaccinated, thanks. It might limit my dating pool significantly though, you know, but, okay, what's it going to take to get an independent committee to look at all this and the way it's supposed to be with no vested financial interest, nobody has patents involved in this. Uh, what's it gonna take for that to happen, Dr. McCullough?

Dr. Peter McCullough: We need courageous people in Washington and Ottawa to call urgent vaccine safety meetings, have independent reviewers, have people opine on the data. Come on, we did this with the "Layatrial." We did this with, um, hormone replacement therapy. We even did this with viagra deaths that were occurring and we managed, we can risk mitigate. I'm not against vaccines. We could actually have a safe vaccine program, but it may be quite selective. And hopefully the vaccines will get easing better. It's not all bad about vacs. It's just that this is really spun out of control. Uh, people are way over their heads. There are people promoting this vaccine program. They have no idea. Um, uh, there are people who have worked in these vaccine centers. You know, they don't even know how to do CPR. I mean, some of these things have been awful. I've seen them try to do CPR in their cars and the people are dying.

Dr. Sam Dubé: Yeah, saw that one.

Dr. Peter McCullough: But in the end, what really wins the day, Dr. Dubé, is when Canadians and Americans just say enough, we're done. You're going to take the vaccine? No, I'm not. Uh, your kids are going to take the vaccine? No, they're not. We're going to vaccinate your kids. No, you're not. And if it takes a parent to go to school and sit with them all day long and say, no you're not going to vaccinate my kid. They don't have to do it.

Dr. Sam Dubé: One of my best friends surprised me the other day, because we've had discussions about this and he's educated in the tech industry and everything. And he just declared that he got the poke and it was like, whoa, wait a minute. I mean, have you not been listening to anything that we've been talking about? He was, uh, bottom line is, I want to travel. Bottom line is I want to travel. And I've heard this from many people. I got to travel, I got to travel. I was contacted by a friend the other day. And he said, this is a personal decision. I'm not his doctor. But he was aware of the findings and he's like, yeah, you know, but I really need to travel for work. And I'm like, have we not discussed this at length? And, you know, and it breaks my heart when people I care about, you know, make this decision seemingly with knowledge. But then there's this fear, you know, whether it's FOMO, you know, uh, whether it's, you know, that I can't earn an income. I mean, some, maybe our public health officials have that fear of not being able to earn income, having to tow the company line, you know when you listen to them speak, months ago they're making sense, now they're not making sense anymore. Do you know even politicians?

Dr. Peter McCullough: Here's a fair way to go, is that, um, the doctor decides who gets the vaccine or not. And I have patients who can't take shots. They can't, it's a medical contraindication. And I write a note. It's like, you know, you can't force peanut butter down the throat of a kid with a peanut allergy. You can't do it. And I'm sorry, it's contraindicated. And there's nobody who can overcome that. There's so much bluster going on. There was, um, the Louisiana State University of Dentistry was like, oh, we're going to mandate vaccines whenever you, and it's like, where's your policy? Oh we don't have a policy. Do you know most places that are mandating vaccines don't have actually an approved vetted, they don't, you ask them for it, they won't provide it. It's actually just bluster. So a typical legal letter that says, send me a copy of your policy because what's going to be adjudicated is going to be the policy. They don't even have it.

In Texas, uh, we actually had, um an order, executive order that says, um, that, uh, you can't inquire about someone's vaccine status, natural immunity counts, you can't say it doesn't. You can't force somebody to have a vaccine and you can't threaten them or lose their job over vaccine, you know, in the government facilities. While, where I went to medical school here in Dallas, UT

Southwestern, um, as I heard via the grapevine that, oh, do you know that they're mandating that the students and the residents take the vaccine? I said, really well, it's a state institution, show me the policy. They're not mandating it. This is all bluster. You know, there's no mandating anything. It's like, show me. And what we need is we need Americans to basically show up and say, listen, show me, oh, I need a vaccine to travel.

No, you can't. Here, I can't take the vaccine. Here's my exemption. And we need doctors to write these exemptions in large numbers because large numbers of people should not take the vaccine. My judgment, if I have a COVID-recovered patient and I know there's no opportunity for benefit and no opportunity of harm: exemption. If I have a poly allergic patient: exemption. I'd have some patients say, you know, doctor, I was sick for three days after their flu shot. That's good enough. Can you imagine COVID-19, it's a hundred times worse than a flu shot. So that's your, sorry exemption. And so doctors ought to be writing exemptions all day long, and we ought to be fronting these exemptions to these blustering people demanding the vaccine, and then we're going to find our way out of it. It will not be a needle in every arm. Anybody listening to this has to understand the needle in every arm is broken. We're going to take down those billboards and burn them because it's not happening.

Dr. Sam Dubé: One last question. I know you've been so generous with your time, uh, Dr. McCullough. Why push the vaccines? I mean, we talk about, you know, conspiracy theories. We talk about, you know, right when you're just, but there's clearly a trail here of evidence. What is going on? Why would they want to mandate, um, a needle in every arm with questionable effect and ingredients for the entire population where it's clearly contraindicated for a good chunk of those people, at the exclusion of other therapies? At the exclusion of seemingly, you know, good signs of common sense. Oh, and as a side, I found a paper from MIT, January 20th, this year, basically talking about, um, viral, uh, visualizations and how the people are using orthodox science to express unorthodox scientific views. And it's like, wait, they're analyzing the same data and coming up with a different conclusion, but using good science and the paper admits that people are using good science and taking matters into their own hands because they want to, you know, see the data and be objective. And they're literally slamming the scientific method because they're so convinced that their narrative is correct. That even good science is not a weapon against their narrative. Do you know what I mean? Did you see that paper?

Dr. Peter McCullough: No, I missed it.

Dr. Sam Dubé: It is unbelievable. Uh, from MIT. I think the, um, the author, um, was, uh, Graham M Jones, MIT visualizations, Viral Visualizations. *How Coronavirus Skeptics Use Orthodox Data Practices to Promote Unorthodox Science Online.* It is a scary, super ironic read. It really is. I recommend that you take a look at it as a scientist, use this. I am sitting there going, I don't know whether to be petrified in fear or laugh my head off, but both, you know, and, uh, this is what we're dealing with. But what do you think is going on here, uh, with trying to get a vaccine in every arm?

Dr. Peter McCullough: All I can tell you is that before the vaccine, I thought it was easier. It was just easier to treat COVID-19. We were getting people through the illness. They were, you know, there are a lot of crises, we're getting through the illness and things, the vaccine from my clinical practice perspective has made things so much worse. Yesterday in our clinic, two patients called in, one person is paralyzed with the vaccine. The other person has some neurologic thing, and we're trying to get neurologist. It is, the vaccine is an unqualified nightmare for the populations. That's the first thing. And so to the people who are listening, who actually know what's going on, they actually know why they want a needle in each arm. What I would say is the following: make something that's better tolerated. If you want a needle in every arm don't make a vaccine, that's the most toxic vaccine in the history of medicine. That's not a good idea for compliance. So for the vaccine stakeholders, the people who are so brilliant to write these patents and you want a needle every arm, do a better job.

Dr. Sam Dubé: Don't give them any ideas Dr. McCullough, come on.

Dr. Peter McCullough: I'm just saying the vaccine is medical crap. It is one of the worst design products I've ever seen. It's awful. The funniest thing is that Johns Hopkins in 2017 had a planning seminar for this. They call people there and they called it the SARS pandemic. They said, listen, there's going to be a pandemic. It's coming. It's going to be a coronavirus is related to MERS and SARS. And it's going to be 2025 to 2028. Well, Kmart.

Dr. Sam Dubé: I've seen the document.

Dr. Peter McCullough: Okay. But the interesting thing is they said there's going to be a drug and it's going to be controversial. I think the name was like "Cavitra" or something or colletra, but it's going to be controversial. But the interesting thing about the drug is that it made people sick. And one of the reasons why it was controversial is because it had side effects. People are vomiting. And anyhow, because of this controversy on the drug, which in a sense is like hydroxychloroquine in terms of a controversial point. Um, and then we're going to use all this and social media and then railroad people into mass vaccination. That was the plan of Johns Hopkins in 2017. The interesting thing is in this case, the drugs aren't the problem. Hydroxy is easy, ivermectin. These are the most safe and they have no side effects and we've had monoclonal antibodies. We can breeze through and prednisone. The drugs are easy. We can treat this so easily. For those of you listening, who are vaccine stakeholders, like you have some plan that you're going to get a needle in every arm, I'm just telling you, it's such an easy problem. If you want it to design a harder problem, design a problem that wouldn't be treatable with drugs. So you'd actually want it, you'd want a problem that we could not treat with drugs, which we can. And then you want a vaccine that was so easily acceptable. That even I would go get one, oh, I'll take one. Well, I need to travel, sure I'll take it. It's like taking a salient shot.

Dr. Sam Dubé: Right? Well, they wouldn't have to suppress all the alternative therapies.

Dr. Peter McCullough: The grant is, if this thing was planned. Like Johns Hopkins says it's planned. It was the worst botched planning in the world. So you made an illness that turned out to be easily treatable and then you try to suppress treatment. That's been a total colossal waste. And so the freedom doctors saved the world anyway. And then on top of that, you make the most toxic vaccine under the sun, and you make everybody sick with blood clots. And whenever you and people are just, you know, they're just, honestly, people are literally ready to just pull their kids out of college and say, forget it and just leave the colleges empty. That's how toxic this vaccine is. So the most interesting thing is, is this really a design? Or is this just one botched thing after another? And the analogy I used the other night on a national media, have you ever, uh, spilled something in the kitchen and it's spreading and you grab some towels, whatever. You try to wipe it up and you make it worse and worse and worse.

This is starting to look like to me, botched bioterrorism. I think that was botched, I think it was bioterrorism going on in this lab. We had involvement with it. Somebody breaks a test tube. It's botched. It spreads all over the world. And now we're trying to clean up the mess since we already have the patents on the bio-terrorism. So, for instance, the Pfizer patent is already there. I mean, this was all planned. Since we already have the patents, let's just try to clean up the mess with a vaccination program and we can make some money as well. All we have to do is keep people in the dark, keeping them fair and locked down. We got to suppress early treatment, whatever we do, don't let Dr. McCullough ever get in charge of things. He'd probably clean up this whole problem by June of last year. Let's not do that. And then let's try to prepare the population for mass vaccination. They get about halfway through the population and it's so toxic, nobody wants this thing anymore. Now they're saying, listen, let's do million dollar raffles. How about a million dollars? You're ready to take a spin with your life. Here's a full Fulbright Scholarship. How about little kids? You don't need a million dollar for kids. Just give them an ice cream cone. Think about it. This is almost like a movie of Batman.

Dr. Sam Dubé: Yeah, exactly. I would just think of the same thing yesterday.

Dr. Peter McCullough: Remember the Joker.

Dr. Sam Dubé: Yes.

Dr. Peter McCullough: The Joker would do something kind of crazy. And then people would be dancing around and they show people in the street are doing something crazy.

Dr. Sam Dubé: And then they get gassed.

Dr. Peter McCullough: And then they get gassed. It's almost like Batman and Robin and they get gassed. And I know Canadians, you guys like to watch these shows too, but bottom line is, Dr. Dubé, what I told Tucker Carlson is something is up. This isn't and it can't be all about COVID. It can't. And I think this is going to be the story of the ages for authors, investigative journalists, others that are going to pull together all the pieces. I would stake my reputation on this. This is not all about COVID.

Dr. Sam Dubé: I want to ask you so many more questions. I want to talk to you more, but I think I'd better let you go, Dr. McCullough. Um, is there anything else you want to say? Just you've got the platform here. I know you've been giving, you know, lots of interviews worldwide, but now here, is there anything else you'd like to say?

Dr. Peter McCullough: I just have two messages. One for doctors and mid-level providers and students, residents, nurses. Uh, we have to bring you out of your trance. Many of you are brainwashed. Many of you are in a trance. Those of you who are injecting pregnant women with no safety data, you're in a trance. Those of you who are injecting little babies, you're in a trance. We're going to bring you out of your trance. You've been a part of wrongdoing and everybody knows this. And the real question is what type of implications will be for you to be complicit in this wrongdoing? The moral authority is to protect the patients. The moral authority is do no harm. That's the moral authority, the moral authority isn't to try to protect against COVID. The vaccine doesn't even do that. The moral authority is safety, safety, safety. That is always going to be the safe haven.

And those of you who want to come out of this good, you better get on the side of safety. For patients, what I'm going to say is, listen, you've had a rough year. This is more than a year. I've had a rough year, been a rough year. This vaccine for most of you is going to make it rougher. And the only way to navigate out of this is start to exercise your voice and say, *no màs*, you don't have to take this vaccine. There's nothing that's ever going to make you take this vaccine. And if the line is the vaccine, draw the line. It's pretty clear. It's pretty clear. It seems to me, the vaccine just came out in December. It's only June right now. What happened in six short months? This thing has become a sociological weapon. It seems to me that this has been thrown out there. This is the line. The vaccine is the line. And the question is what side of the line you're going to be on? I've talked to now a lot of regretful people. Now on the McCullough report, which is on America out loud radio.

Dr. Sam Dubé: I was going to mention.

Dr. Peter McCullough: That's coming up. Yeah, that's coming up. I interviewed Carrie Savage. He's a very prominent infectious disease doctor. He's older. He's at risk for COVID-19. All he did all year long was take care of COVID patients. He knows what he's talking about. And he's someone who took the COVID-19 vaccine. And now based on the safety data, he's regretful. So those of you who are on the line of taking the vaccine, and if you have some remorse or regret, get on the right side of the line, those of you who've um, uh, not had the vaccine. You know, there may be a few of you talking to good doctors and I'd be happy to talk to any one of you regarding whether or not your risk profile is that you should get the vaccine. You know, a lot of us are on this side of the line because we've already had the virus. Honestly, I've already had it. I've already had a dose of bioterrorism. I know what it feels like. I know what it feels like to not breathe. Listen, I had that spike protein in me. I had risks of blood clotting and everything else. So those of you who got through the virus, you know that's a badge of courage, if you will.

Dr. Sam Dubé: I had it March of last year.

Dr. Peter McCullough: Yeah. So we're done. We're done. I mean, do you have anything in your mind where you could think that there's any reason that you would take the vaccine?

Dr. Sam Dubé: No. Knowing what I know? No, absolutely not. No, absolutely not. And what's shame now is with the, uh, Dr. Fauci emails coming out, there's a whole bunch of redacted stuff that hasn't been seen. That Indian paper that came out was January of 2020. I remember seeing that paper, I read the paper, three days later, it's gone. I think they were among the first to say, hey, this is a bioengineered, you know genetically engineered virus guys, seriously. And then no apology. Just, we're retracting, we will publish someday bye. That was it. That Indian team. And I don't know what happened to the paper, but they sounded the alarm a long time ago, but apparently Chinese pressure, they had to retract it.

Dr. Peter McCullough: I'm going to come out on a panel tonight, I guess it'll be too late for the viewers, but on the Ingraham Angle and the working group that I formed is called C 19. And we're about a thousand people strong, we're on national TV every night. There's Panda, they're worldwide. They're even bigger. The COVID for medical ethics in the UK. Uh, we have a big voice out there and, um, and we are bringing truth to the public. You know, our show on Laura Ingraham is going to be about these emails, uh, and others opine on it. Mine was, um, more of the medical side of the panel, but, you know, an email I saw yesterday was something like this. And it went into the, um, the NIH, uh, NIAED director. It said, hey, Tony, how did you engineer that HIV into the spike protein? You know, it was almost like it was like a fun science experiment. You know, it's like, really, that's a fun science experiment. Now, you and I got to experience some of this. And now everybody getting the vaccines, going to get to experience a little bit of fun of this size vaccine. I think Americans and Canadians will develop a sense of rage when they realize the malfeasance and the wrongdoing by those in a position of authority, they are going to be enraged and it's going to be for decades in the future.

Dr. Sam Dubé: I hope so. Dr. Peter McCullough, I want to thank you so much again, website americaoutloud.com go to shows. Go to the McCullough report. You were asked to produce that show and I've listened to several episodes and it's very informative. Thank you so much for that. And as I mentioned before, you're doing great work, it was an honour to have you on our show. And I hope to speak to you again in the near future and good luck and stay safe because I'm paranoid. So please stay in touch. On behalf of myself, Dr. Sam Dubé, and the *Toronto Business Journal*. Thank you so much Dr. Peter McCullough for being on our show, once again.

APPENDIX 3

Vaccine Legal Expert Discusses CBC and Other Propaganda on COVID-19 Injection

DR. SAM DUBÉ: HELLO, DR. Sam Dubé here once again for the *Toronto Business Journal*. And we're joined here today by Mary S. Holland, Esquire. She is the president and general counsel of Children's Health Defense, and she for 20 years was a professor in the law schools of Columbia, NYU. So Mary, thank you so much for joining us today.

Mary Holland: My pleasure.

Dr. Sam Dubé: Mary, why was Children's Health Defense funded or founded?

Mary Holland: So it actually was first founded under a different name, Sam. It was called the World Mercury Project, and Robert F. Kennedy Jr., um, became the director of World Mercury Project. And he, as an environmental lawyer, had long been concerned about the environmental impacts of mercury. And over time, he became aware that a critical, uh, preservative that was being used in childhood vaccines was thimerosal, which was half ethyl mercury by weight. But the more that he and his team became involved in looking at mercury, the more they understood that there were many other toxic exposures to children that were causing this terrible epidemic that we have of childhood chronic disease. So over 54% of children in the United States have some kind of serious chronic health condition, over half. It's just horrifying. So we decided in, I guess, 2017 to change the name of World Mercury Project to Children's Health Defense.

And we focus not only on the toxic exposures through vaccines, but other things like pesticides, like, um, wireless technology, like, um, glyphosate. Um, like fluoride in water. So we're looking at all kinds of environmental exposures and climate change, actually. That's another thing that we're looking at. We're looking at all of the exposures that we believe are contributing to the ill health of our children. But in fact, in the last year, plus during the COVID pandemic, a lot of our attention necessarily has been on COVID, uh, because it's changed, you know, virtually everything, including the world for children. So we've put a lot of attention on that and, I'm happy to talk more about that.

Dr. Sam Dubé: Absolutely. So that's one of the priorities of our meeting today in our interview, Mary. Um, if we could just give a little background, uh, some context here for this interview, could you explain to our viewers about the vaccine act, and I believe that was signed, was it the Reagan administration? Was it 86, if I recall correctly, in 86 and how would it indemnifies, um, companies, uh, vaccine manufacturers and such. Could you please elucidate.

Mary Holland: You bet. So let's just take a little step back to, you know, vaccines have been around for a long time, and their primary use from like the 17 hundreds to the end of the 18 hundreds in Europe and the United States in particular was against smallpox. And when they were being used against smallpox, they were basically used for the whole population. And the landmark decision from in the US Supreme court relates to a smallpox epidemic and the use of a mandate in Massachusetts statewide, but by the 1950s, vaccines. So, by the 1950s, vaccines were primarily being used for children. The notion was that they would be preventing infectious diseases for children and going forward. So first we saw the diphtheria tetanus pertussis vaccines come in wide use, the polio vaccines in the fifties come in wide use, but by the sixties, the early sixties also then the measles mumps rubella vaccine came into wide use.

So by the early eighties, there were a lot of lawsuits against vaccine manufacturers, against the pharmaceutical industry, because it was being observed that certain children were developing severe side effects from vaccines, particularly the pertussis vaccine. It was a wholesale pertussis in the DPT shots. So children were developing intellectual disability. What is today called autism; cerebral palsy and there were deaths. And so, um, by, so in the early 1980s, negotiation started in the Senate in the United States Congress, and they were between the pharmaceutical industry, the medical industry and parents of vaccine-injured children. And in 1986, they came to a kind of negotiated settlement of the 1986 National Childhood Vaccine Injury Act. And that law that Congress passed and Reagan signed, although he had a lot of objections to it, it acknowledged that some children die and are permanently injured by vaccines. That was, if you will, the good news.

And we thought the good news or the parents of vaccine-injured children thought that the good news was they were going to set up a no fault compensation program. So if you know, the evidence suggested that your kid was harmed, and if your kid fell in this table, that said, if you develop, you know, Aflaxen within four hours, or if you develop seizures within three days, you would sort of, the idea was you'd automatically get compensated by this vaccine injury compensation program. Um, it worked a little bit at the very beginning for people who'd been injured by DPT and MMR in particular, but over time, giving any industry, but particularly giving pharma, essentially liability protection, right? You don't get to sue pharma. You go to this government conversation program that was a green light, right. We can mandate it on the front end. We have liability protection on the backend.

Hallelujah, full speed ahead.

So, you know, by the early two thousands, we had 16, in most states, we had 16 mandated vaccines. It was up to 72 doses for children because certain things like DPT have five doses. MMR is two, going on three. Hepatitis B became multiple doses. So 72 doses. And, um, you know, we had, there's a lot, a lot, a lot of problems with the injury compensation program. Very few cases on the whole get compensated. The proof that's required is daunting. The table of injuries, which would lead to presumptive compensation, has not been expanded. Um, especially in the early two-thousands, there was a very problematic proceeding called the omnibus autism proceeding that found, I believe wrongly, that vaccines don't cause autism. So that's a problem.

In COVID the situation is actually even worse, Sam, in COVID because the vaccines and other products are Emergency Use Authorization; they're not actually approved, licensed, or federally recommended. They fall within an even more, um, restrictive, uh, law, which is called the prep act from 2005 that was introduced after 9/11 and after an anthrax scare. And that law basically creates an even more insular, no liability tribunal within the US health and human services department for compensation. And sadly, Sam, I'm not going to hold my breath for literally any compensation to victims of COVID vaccines at this point.

Dr. Sam Dubé: Wow. So because of the original vaccine act, basically they're taking their responsibility away from the vaccine manufacturers because they insisted on having some sort of agreement because there were claims for vaccine injuries among parents. And so they said, well, look, we don't want to make, keep making vaccines here. We need some kind of protection. So you're saying the government took over. Is that where the funds came from to basically, uh, compensate these families and the children that were, uh, proven to be vaccine injured? And this was actually kept pretty hush hush by the media. Is that correct?

Mary Holland: Well, I'm not sure it was hush hush back in 1986. I think they talked about it as, you know, a great success. This was the first public experiment in tort reform. Um, but, um, yes, this fund for the injuries is, um, achieved through a 75 cent fee on each dose of vaccine. So for instance, you know, the MMR is basically three vaccines, so that would be $2.25 cents that's paid by the consumer into this vaccine fund. So that fund has several billion dollars. The injury compensation program has paid out over $4 billion to injured, um, victims of vaccine injury. Um, so Pharma doesn't really feel any pain, right? It's not their money. Um, and in theory, Sam, the '86 Act did permit, uh, people to actually file in court, but uh what year was it? I think it's a 2011

Supreme court decision narrowed access to federal courts, uh, well to all courts, um, in the case of vaccine injury.

So when the '86 Act was passed, it was sort of an open question, whether, um, you could sue if a vaccine was designed in a defective way and my reading of it and the reading of many people is that the vaccine act left that open, that people could file first in the injury compensation program if they lost. But if there was a fundamental flaw with the vaccine, they could go and hold pharma accountable, but it was decided in 2011, I believe in a case called Bruesewitz vs Wyeth that now the only agency that can retract a badly designed vaccine is the FDA. And you cannot bring a design defect claim to any court, state, or federal. So that basically then meant complete liability protection for these vaccines. Well, virtually I shouldn't say that, not complete, virtually complete.

And so the biggest opening still to go after Pharma is related to fraud. And so Children's Health Defense in conjunction with uh private law firms is pursuing Merck, uh, for their Gardasil vaccine, their human papilloma virus vaccine on the theory that it is fraud, uh, and a few other claims that they failed to warn that, that there were other things, but basically that they defrauded the federal government, they defraud consumers, um, with their claims that it prevents cervical cancer and that it doesn't have severe side effects.

Dr. Sam Dubé: Right. And, uh, you know that's something I definitely read up about. So basically, is it true then that if you tried to, uh, take, um, someone to court for, you know, claim for a vaccine injury that you were actually taking the Department of Justice to court, that it was them that was taking up the fight?

Mary Holland: That you have to. So today, if your child is injured or if an adult actually is injured. Let's say I'm injured by, let's say I take a flu vaccine, which I do not, but let's say I take a flu vaccine and I'm injured, I become paralyzed. I would have to, within three years, file a petition with the vaccine injury compensation program. And, um, that claim would, I would be suing Health and Human Services and Health and Human Services would be represented by the Department of Justice. Now, the good news again, under the 86 act is I actually would be able to find a lawyer and the lawyer's fees would be paid for out of this compensation program. So my rights would be better protected in this injury compensation program, in the countermeasures injury compensation program, which covers COVID vaccines and COVID drugs.

In that case, I would not get any legal fees. I would have no live hearing. I would have only the opportunity to present documents. I would have no access to review by a court. This injury compensation program, actually the cases do then go to the federal court, the Court of Federal Claims. And then they go to the Court of Appeals for the federal circuit. Under COVID situation, the countermeasures injury compensation program, You can only appeal within health and human services itself. And then you can appeal to the court of federal claims, but it's, you know, it's virtually impossible.

Dr. Sam Dubé: So a far more challenging path given the crosstalk.

Mary Holland: Much much much more.

Dr. Sam Dubé: Okay, so you spoke to that already. Now, are there any other implications or stipulations of the emergency use authorization that our viewers should know about?

Mary Holland: Yes, absolutely. So world over, the COVID shots are only today in any country of the world that I'm aware of. They're only given emergency use authorization. So what does that mean? In the United States that means that the food and drug administration that's responsible for foods and drugs, which includes what are called biologics. Vaccines are considered to be not drugs, but biologics. It means that the FDA has to review them. And because all of these COVID shots were done on such a fast paced schedule, they did not have the standard level of evidence available to determine whether they are in fact safe and effective. So the FDA has not said that these products are safe and effective. The FDA has said they may be safe and effective. The FDA has said there is no adequate available alternative to this product. That is a claim about which we need to be very skeptical. I'm happy to talk about that further.

But the criteria for the EUA is that there's no available alternative. This is the best we know, it may be effective. And the federal statute, Sam, says that an individual must have the right to accept or refuse this medical intervention. And the statute says there may be consequences to the decision to accept or refuse i.e the person might have medical side effects if they take it, they might be more susceptible to disease if they don't take it. But our reading of that federal statute regarding the EUA status is that the consequences they're talking about are medical consequences. They're not talking about dishonorable discharge from the military, termination from your job, exclusion from your University. In our view, all of those things are not in accordance with federal law, but that's being actively litigated right now. And the first big decision that just came down from a federal court in Texas, regarding employees who were fired at Houston hospital, the decision at the moment is that the hospital has that right.

You don't have a constitutional right to a job. Um, if people don't want to take these products, they can go elsewhere to work. Uh, we don't read it that way. We know that lawyer is going to appeal. Um, but, uh, that's the view of a court right now that, um, you know, that law is not about a private actor. Uh, it doesn't give them a private right of action. We don't agree with that. The reason we don't agree with that is because coming out of World War Two, where we saw medical atrocities. The world embraced the Nuremberg Code. And the first principle of the Nuremberg Code is the consent of the individual to any experiment is absolutely essential, absolutely essential, no exceptions. That principle has actually been expanded over the last 75 years, so that it applies to virtually all medical interventions, and UNESCO put out in 2005 a Universal Declaration on Bioethics and Human Rights.

And it says the interest of science and the interest of society are not sufficient ever to decide the issue of informed consent. The issue, the right of informed consent rests in the individual. So from our perspective, the decision in the federal court in Texas is wrong-headed. There must be this very strong prohibition against forcing individuals, coercing individuals into, um, taking an experimental medical product. Uh, but the court said, you know, they just have to leave their jobs. I think that's a wrong decision, but you know, we're going to see lots of cases on this Sam. We're going to see tenured professors being terminated from their positions. We're going to be seeing people who are just shy of their pension being terminated. We're going to see students being thrown out of colleges, assuming that this train keeps going in the same direction.

We at children's health defense are fighting this train very hard because we believe it's extremely dangerous. And we believe that the information that's being put out there, that these products are safe and effective, that there's no long-term effect, you know, side effects, that there are no serious side effects. Now that's just false. I mean, that's just false information.

Dr. Sam Dubé: Right. And, uh, in fact, uh, before we get to that, and that's going to be the meat and potatoes of this interview here, um, because we definitely have something big to talk about there, uh, especially relevant to Canadians, um, is, uh, you talked about the skepticism, uh, concerning the declaration that there are no alternative, reasonable alternative treatments. So can we please speak to this because I've definitely done a lot of interviews about this.

Mary Holland: Yes. I know you have. I saw that you interviewed Dr. Corey and others and it's so important. So our view, Sam, is that, um, powers that be, people in the US government in scientific agencies, the national institutes of health, the FDA, the centers for dispensing, the centers for disease control, they knowingly suppressed information about hydroxychloroquine and ivermectin in particular, drugs that are safe, effective, not patented long in use, known to have a very low risk profile. Those things were intentionally suppressed worldwide in order to clear the path for these experimental vaccines to come into the marketplace. And we know that there have been long-term investments in this mRNA technology, which industry loves because their view is that it's cheap. It's easy to manufacture on this huge scale, and it's easy to tweak, right? They're already talking about tweaking this for the variants.

So we know that they were looking for the opportunity to bring this new technology, this mRNA technology into the marketplace. And apparently the EUAs regarding COVID-19 were the ideal pathway. And so from our perspective, great interventions were made to protect that pathway. In fact, from our perspective based on information from people like Dr. Peter McCullough and Dr. Quarry and Dr. Laurie and others.

Dr. Sam Dubé: And now Dr. Malone, even, Dr. Robert Malone even.

Mary Holland: Dr. Malone, exactly Dr. Malone, thank you. 80 to 85% of the deaths from COVID-19 could have been prevented. That's an extraordinary indictment of, um, the health, the public health officials in charge.

Dr. Sam Dubé: I'm so glad you said that because it's become so apparent. And if you watch, uh, uh, just going back to Dr. Robert Malone on, uh, I'll just say this DB Wire Up High, uh, he did an hour and 40 minute long interview, and, uh, he expresses deep concern. And this is a gentleman who's been involved in development of the RNA technology since the late eighties and saw it all unfold. It was supposedly, originally supposed to be used for gene therapy. And then he decided, well, let's use it for the V instead, right? So this is what we're talking about here, is these experts are all coming out and, uh, and alarm bells are going off and saying, you know, especially with the early treatments, like what is going on here, and you already alluded to the long term, potential long-term side effects and um the safety, and especially with regards to, uh, children and pregnant women.

So this is something we really need to address. There's so many questions and you know what? It is so refreshing speaking to you as a senior legal expert on this. And you're so clear, and you're so objective, and I want to thank you so much for coming on our show today, and for making this, you know, very palatable and understandable to our viewers. There's a lot of things out there that we don't know. And I have to say this, especially among Canadians, you know, we're a gentle people. We're a proud people. We're a nice people and we help others. We really do. I love being Canadian. You know what I mean? And this is not to denigrate any other nation, but I'm finding now that our natural gentle tendencies, we don't speak up. And we often, we say, well we should trust this organization. You know, we're not Americans, we're not Americans you know. We don't have this red versus blue in all this.

Wait a minute, guys, I have a document here that we need to really go over because there are some serious, serious concerns of what's being stated in this Canadian Broadcasting Corporation document, that was published on June the 13th, 2021. So we'll address that in a moment, but let's get to VAERS and the CDC statistics, which are prevalent on your site and this whole idea of, you know, no long-term side effects and deaths attributed to vaccines. Let's address that issue. I'll let you take that away, Mary.

Mary Holland: Sure. So, um, I want your viewers to know that Children's Health Defense has a free publication that comes out every day, called the Defender. So go to our website, www childrenshealthdefense.org, and sign up for the Defender, if you want information on these topics. Um, so every Friday, for many months now, we've been coming out with the latest information that's published by. It's a joint, the latest information in VAERS, the vaccine adverse event reporting system. So that's a system that was put in place by the 1986 national vaccine injury, uh, national childhood vaccine injury act, um, to cover, uh, injuries from vaccines. You know, it's important that doctors and consumers and everybody know what that information is.

Uh, it's jointly run by the FDA and the CDC. It's a program with lots of problems, but it's the only thing that's really accessible to the public about what are the adverse events, what are the side effects, and we take the information because it's in a very easy to grasp format from the National Vaccine Information Center, a colleague of ours, another organization that's very focused on vaccine safety. So the various data that was released this past Friday, shows a total of 387,087 adverse events for all age groups, including 6,113 deaths and 31,240 serious injuries between December 14th when these vaccines came on the market, June 18th. Sam we've never seen anything like this. So the VAER System, as I said, is very problematic. It's what's called a passive reporting system. Doctors don't face any penalties if they don't report.

Most doctors don't recognize what is a vaccine injury. Consumers don't know that they do have the right to report to VAERS. Even though the CDC says that they follow up on deaths and serious injuries, we know from many people who have reported that that's not always the case. Scientific, several scientific papers, including one funded by the US government. The health and human services have found that literally under 1% of vaccine injuries are typically reported. So HHS contracted with the Harvard Pilgrim Health Maintenance Organization, and they did machine learning to see if people got a vaccine, what did they show up with three months later? Or what did they show up with two weeks later? And they found in that, that under 1% of the vaccine injuries were being reported. And at that point the HHS, Health and Human Services said, thank you very much. We're not interested in continuing this study. This was a gross indictment. The US government does have other tracking systems and they do discuss them at CDC and FDA meetings, they are public, but we the public don't have access to that data, but this data is extremely troubling. And it shows us that there is a level of injury from these experimental COVID shots. That's unprecedented from other vaccines. And I've been in this field for 20 years. I mean, we were deeply troubled with vaccine injury well before COVID, but typically, Sam, VAERS has about 200 deaths reported a year. We know that's a gross under count, but it's 2000, 200 are reported a year. In a half a year for COVID shots they're reporting six, over 6,000 deaths. Now, granted they're vaccinating far more people because they're vaccinating the adult population.

But, there's 387,000 adverse events reported. And we know, even if you say, okay, maybe COVID shot, there's more attention. Maybe doctors are more concerned. They're actually reporting. Maybe it's not 1%. Maybe they're reporting 10%. If you said they're reporting 10%, that would be over 3 million adverse events. And honestly, Sam, my sense is that's probably right. I mean, if you look at, you know, social media, which is being centered, but if you just talk to people, did you get a shot? Did you have any side effects? I mean, companies are saying you get a day off, you get three days off, you know, because of your side effects. I mean, I've been in groups of people and said, do you know anybody who's died after they got a COVID shot and a lot of hands go up. So these are not proven safe and effective. These are not typical vaccines. They have not undergone 10 years, which is typical for vaccine clinical trials before they are put out to the public. This is gone through at the moment, six months, six months in clinical trials.

Dr. Sam Dubé: And this is it. And I believe in the initial clinical trials, there were no children, there were no pregnant women. Uh, and there were no, uh, elderly, uh, as far as I know, they were taking it.

Mary Holland: That's correct Sam. So, you know, they're now doing clinical trials in all those groups. And I was just, I do a podcast once a week with Polly Tommey, who is one of the producers of *Vaxxed* and, um, *Vaxxed II: The People's Truth*. And, uh, we were talking yesterday, they're now doing clinical trials in two-month-olds to six-month-olds. Uh, and they also are doing clinical trials in pregnant women. I mean, the vision here, we have to look at the bigger picture. The vision here is literally pre-cradle to grave vaccination. That is what powers that be want to see. And we're starting to see this, you know, oh, you know, those two doses that you got so that you can be protected. Well, it's not enough. You've got to come back for your vaccine against the variants.

And literally we've been reading articles that talk about, you know, vaccination every season before you get to get together with your family members for, you know, holidays. I mean, it's an extraordinary vision about tinkering with the human body. And, um, this vision extends to, you know, we now live in this world of the internet of things, right? Your refrigerator, your car, your thermostat are all connected to the internet. Well, now there's serious discussion, Sam, about the internet of bodies and really being able to, you know, make money and manipulate the human body in ways that commodify the body.

Dr. Sam Dubé: You know, given the way the pandemic unfolded and especially the reliance on the PCR test and no good explanation as to why they were going with 45 cycles when it's quite well known that anything above 24 of it starts to become very unreliable when you're amplifying the very small samples and strands of RNA and DNA that are found in a person's, uh, body. Um, you know, you can amplify to the point where anything, as Kerry Mullis said, the inventor of the test, is anything becomes something to talk about. Right? And so no good explanation there. And so one of the foundations of this pandemic and the numbers of cases is, you know, basically just counting every positive test as a case, and then expanding that with this whole contact tracing, especially in the U.S. where it's like, wow, this person has got...

Now we got to look at their contacts and say, okay, there are also, you know, cases now, and you can get counted multiple times and then death certificates in the hospital. I've had, you know, secondhand, firsthand knowledge of this, of seeing these things filled out and hearing, you know, there were six deaths in my immediate circle. Okay. Most of them, uh, uh, elderly or infirm over COVID, but none of them had COVID. None of them had tested positive for COVID. Okay. Three of them died in isolation, in the hospital, one died at home. All right. And he was not much older than me, and he died at home needing a surgery. All right. So, this is one thing that motivates me. We can talk to so many other things. We haven't even talked about the possibility of antibody dependent enhancement.

We haven't talked about the variants. We haven't talked about the studies showing that people who have been fully vaccinated may experience a much higher incidence of being, you know, at experiencing adverse effects upon getting infected again. We're finding, there's a study that recently came out of Israel showing that half the people. I mean, most of the country there is vaccinated. So that, that makes sense. Um, and they're getting re-infected and they're getting really adverse effects. I'm very concerned about, you know, the so-called low vitamin D season or flu season coming up. And if they're going to blame it on the un-vaccinated, if they're going to blame it on variants, if they're going to say, like you were saying, we're going to need more vaccines boosters or regular schedule. This is a path that's very difficult to turn from. And slowly but surely we're hearing from people.

I interviewed Dr. Kory back in December, we didn't get a lot of use. We got shadow banned and many people since then have expressed their concern, Dr. Peter McCullough. And now the latest Dr. Robert Malone, who's been there since allegedly, you know, the beginning of the RNA technology expressing his concern. And, you know, we're getting information, even from the so-called public health officials that is changing. I mean, look at the Fauci emails. Okay. And I mean, we don't even have to go there, but I want to touch on one really important thing right now. And then we can use that as a springboard for the rest of it. And that is the World Health Organization's guidelines regarding children. Can you tell us exactly what happened there? Because I could have sworn there was a statement there um not recommending giving the vaccine. Uh, and I think it was the Pfizer vaccine, but I'm not a hundred percent sure now because I didn't screenshot it, to children, but could you please tell us in the chronology of what actually happened?

Mary Holland: Absolutely. So last week on Monday, we became aware that a document allegedly from June 3rd was put on the world health organization website that's that recommended against giving children 12 to 15 COVID vaccines and saying, it's not ready for children at this time, at this moment. Um, because remember, in the US, as of May, emergency use authorization was granted for Pfizer vaccines for 12 to 15 year olds. So it was interesting that on Monday, last week, the world health organization came out with contradictory advice to the United States, to the FDA saying it's not ready for prime time for kids 12 to 15. Last Friday, the Centers for Disease Control's advisory committee on immunization practices, their sort of vaccine gurus had a meeting. And by Friday, the world health organization had dropped its line saying, not at this moment for kids. And it replaced it by, it is suitable to give to children, no rationale for the change.

And we actually did screenshot that Sam, and that's on the Defender and we show the two versions. That's not science, Sam. That is marketing. There's no rationale. They go from one day, don't do it for kids. And the next day go right ahead. No logic, no rationale. So we don't know exactly what happened. It would be very interesting to know what were the discussions between the World Health Organization and the Centers for Disease Control. But, uh, you know, now they're recommending it for kids. So that meeting last Friday, I actually sat through all five hours of the meeting. And, um, we had Dr. Merrill Nass, um, an accomplished physician in this area do live blogging of it again on the Defender website. And, um, you know, this meeting was called to discuss the risks that's now evident, not only from Israel, but in the US that young men in particular, but young people are at risk when they get COVID shots of what they call myocarditis and pericarditis, inflammation of the heart muscle, or the muscle around the heart. And obviously that can kill you. And we had a story about a beautiful 18 year old girl at Northwestern who got myocarditis. They tried to do a heart transplant and she died, and we just published another story about a beautiful 13 year old boy. He gets the vaccine, the Pfizer, two days later, he's dead.

So Sam, these are real deaths. You know, you can't fake a death. Like there's no psychosomatic death, it just doesn't exist. And they're acknowledging now, they're putting a warning label for children on the Pfizer vaccine for 12 to 15, that it can cause inflammation of the heart. Sam children are not, there have been deaths in children from COVID. There have been, there've been a couple hundred. There's good evidence, there's good science showing that that number just as for adults is likely inflated, but children are at exceptionally low risk of COVID, exceptionally low. It seems that for most children, if they get it it's asymptomatic, or if they get it, there are mild symptoms. There are a few cases of, they call it MSC, there's a multi-system inflammatory disorder, but it's very rare. And it's typically children with underlying conditions who maybe do need other precautions. Maybe those children really do need to be isolated. But, um, the idea that the benefits outweigh the risks, which is what the CDC, and now the WHO are saying, I think that your viewers should exercise a great deal of skepticism about that.

And as we didn't get into yet, but how can they rationally say that there are no long-term effects and know that. This is the first time in a broad population, mRNA vaccines have ever been used. They have been used for, I guess, over 10 years for cancer patients, as gene therapy. Those are people who are absolutely facing a likelihood of death from their illness. Um, and so using something like this intervention, of course, you're going to tolerate a very high level of risk. For healthy children, parents should accept virtually no risk. Their children are at exceptionally low risk. So if they're telling you explicitly, there is a risk of heart inflammation, you should be very skeptical that this is something that you believe is valuable for your child.

Dr. Sam Dubé: Especially since you know, these conditions, myocarditis in particular, we can't predict how it's going to affect someone throughout their life. As Dr. Roger Hopkinsons spoke to very effectively, you know, heart muscle dies, heart cells, muscle cells die. Myo is muscle. Cardio is heart and itis is inflammation. It's a very generic term, but this is a very serious condition. And you may never be the same after that. You may never be the same. And we're not. We're talking about teenagers, adolescent children.

Mary Holland: We ran a story about a boy who developed myocarditis and he's hospitalized. And the doctors are telling them it's at least two years, he was a star athlete, at least two years to recover. And the boy says I would have rather had COVID and he's right. He's right. I mean, and who knows if the doctors are right, it's going to be two years. They don't know.

Dr. Sam Dubé: Oh my goodness. Was he the, uh, the basketball player, the 17 year old basketball player? Um, yeah. Yeah. And I mean, he was the picture of health. He was the picture of playing basketball hours and hours a day. And it's just heartbreaking. It was heartbreaking, heartbreaking for his mom who comes from a family of physicians, who was insisting that he take the vaccine and now feels very, very guilty because he didn't want to take it. And she feels so guilty because she was accepting.

Mary Holland: You know, this is so hard, Sam, because you are a physician and we are trained and we want to trust our physicians. We need to trust people in life, you can't get through life without trusting some people and we want, and we need to trust people in authority. And the sad reality here is the vast majority of doctors have no idea what they are telling their patients to do. And they are leading their patients astray.

Dr. Sam Dubé: And, you know, my heart goes out to the physicians as well. I may take some flack for this, but I'll tell ya, we're human. You know, we're human. And we have thoughts and feelings and anxieties and concerns and personal concerns. And, you know, we train really, really hard. I went to med school with a wonderful crop of people and my heart goes out to them.

Mary Holland: I [40:21 inaudible]. I mean we at children's health defense are working with physicians. Physicians are instrumental to solving these problems, but the sad reality Sam, is the doctors do have a responsibility.

Dr. Sam Dubé: Absolutely, absolutely.

Mary Holland: Most of them, I'm sorry to say, are shirking those responsibilities. They advise their patients that this is experimental. There are no long-term data. This has not been proven safe and effective. There's far more that we don't know then that we do know, and most physicians are not telling their patients.

Dr. Sam Dubé: And nowhere was, I absolving anyone from responsibility because I'm [40:58 inaudible] position.

Mary Holland: I know and do feel for the doctors.

Dr. Sam Dubé: You know, and they, you know, the message is you got to scrutinize, you got to validate, you got to question, you got to stick to your Hippocratic oath, uh, your tenets of, you know, informed consent and do no harm. Informed consent and do no harm. Stick to those, you know. And it's not about playing ball. It's not about a consensus, you know, that may or may. I mean, look, I mean, the science is starting to become very clear, right? So, you know, there's some things that, you know, we probably don't have time to address here, but I asked you to take a look at an article published by the Canadian Broadcasting Corporation. And we've both printed it out. This was June 13th. We're currently at the end of June, 2021 and in a heat wave. And you're much further south than me. This is why your hair is blowing. I just want to inform our viewers that it's not, uh, you know, any other effect there, besides the fans.

Mary Holland: Yes it's hot here.

Dr. Sam Dubé: You Know, we are a 30 degrees plus Celsius right now. And I'm in over the 49th parallel. Okay. And you are well, well below that. So I can only imagine how hot it is for you down where you are, but this article was called "Busting Myths About Vaccination and Why Experts Say It's Essential to Our Return to Normal." So this was produced, published in response to what's perceived to be vaccine hesitancy among, um, you know, a good percentage of the population, especially those who've, you know, um, many people have had a first dose and are now really, really delaying that second dose. So there's some things here said where they make these gross generalize, uh, statements and, uh, you know, they start, the article in saying that the more people are vaccinated, the less opportunity virus has to mutate and wreak havoc, health experts say. Okay, which health experts, right? I mean, you can definitely cherry pick, but the really concerning thing is the statement in there. And I'll just synopsize that there's no proof of long-term vaccine side effects and that the spike protein is completely safe. Both of which we know is not.

Mary Holland: This is false. So I mean, doctors like Dr. Whelan, we published his letter to the FDA that he wrote to the FDA in December saying spike protein is what's causing the inflammation. That's the problem with COVID. And so we're now injecting that into people. That's simply false information. And I just think on its face, Sam, it's a bold untrue to say, there are no long-term health effects. How can they possibly say that?

Dr. Sam Dubé: Exactly.

Mary Holland: It's never been used in a healthy population ever before ever. So that's just on its face a false statement, which should make people then question everything they're being told.

Dr. Sam Dubé: You know, and here talking about, whoa, we›re providing incentives to fully vaccinated people, you know, coercion, maybe we could use another word there, you know, and you just addressed that already. And, uh, the lack of informed consent, you know, especially with an article like this, I mean, I have highlighted so much in here and we just really won›t make the time to go over all this, but I›m talking about the speed of the development. You know, what did the emergency use authorization allow? I believe initially, no animal studies. They could bypass animal studies?

Mary Holland: In the Moderna trials, they skipped over animal trials. They did it explicitly because it was such an emergency. Um, you know, the animals that were used in the AstraZeneca trials, I believe became very ill. Um, so you know, this article that you suggested, which I agree is important because it's from the Canadian Broadcasting Corporation, uh, you know, it addresses speed, effectiveness, ingredients, um, necessity, side effects, blood clots, and long-term effects. And they try basically, I mean, let's be real Sam, this is a marketing piece. This is trying to convince people, go get the vaccine. We were told to tell you to go get your vaccine and we'll get some kind of bonus. If you go get your vaccine. So go get your vaccine. That's basically what this says and sad to say, you know, that's not true.

Dr. Sam Dubé: In claiming to address misinformation, they are providing massive misinformation, and we've already addressed many of the points, uh, in this publication, in this article. We've already addressed many of the falsities and the misinformation here. So, you know, talking about unprecedented global cooperation in research to get this out to people on the market saying that there were no shortcuts, there was only an expediting. What, no shortcuts? Many experts have come out to say that that's not true at all. There were many shortcuts and now anyone getting the injection is in phase three, right? So as you said, eloquently at the beginning, the FDA did not approve these injections. They allowed them, they allowed them.

Mary Holland: They may be safe and effective. That's all that's out there. And it's often mis-characterized even by, you know, CDC.

Dr. Sam Dubé: While still maintaining the same standards for safety and efficacy, really, really well. You're going to have to debate VAERS and you know what, they do, they do debate VAERS. But the fact still remains statistically, when you compare the number of VAERS report pre or the equivalent VAERS reports pre-pandemic, with during the pandemic, um, it's just the numbers show that there's a vast, difference in the number of reports. And then when you get, uh, Dr. Peter McCullough, who's done these kinds of verifications themselves. He said, they're claiming that they went over the initial 1600 reports of mortality, and they claimed that while there's nothing there, it's not due to the vaccine. Really. You went over all the patient information and the histories and the death certificates. And like we see there's literally video footage of people in cars seizing after their vaccines and dying shortly thereafter.

Like how can they make this kind of claim? You know? So I know you have to go soon. So is there anything else that we can address here? Um, they're claiming that, uh, wow. That, I mean, this is, I urge people to even look at this and compare and refer back to our interview. A harmless piece of spike protein, they refer to a harmless piece of spike protein. We knew about the S1 subunit spike protein. It is not a neutral antigen. It is not a neutral piece of protein that your body develops antibodies to. It has properties on its own that cause damage. It is toxic. And we don't know the extent to which it is toxic. Um, we do know how it starts to accumulate now, thanks to Dr. Byram Bridle, talking about this, opening that up with a Japanese verification and you know, so is there, I know you need to go, is there anything else that we can talk to regarding, um, the, I guess propaganda that is being used.

Mary Holland: But it is propaganda. It's a marketing pitch. And I think we have to recognize that the media has colluded, is cooperating with these governmental pushes. This is a worldwide effort to vaccinate every person on the planet. And I think we have to be very skeptical about that. This is an emergency product. It's not understood what its long-term effects are. It can't be understood. And why are they pushing this so hard? Why are they coercing people? Why are they incentivizing people? COVID was not so terrible. It was on par with the severe seasonal flu. So people need to first step up and say, what the hell is going on? And there are a lot of possible explanations. I don't have the crystal ball, but people have, they have to think, right. Question authority; think critically, this is not normal. This is not normal. And I urge people to read The Defender, go to Children's Health Defense, and sign up for The Defender. We're trying to answer these questions every day, we're trying to put out… information. We give citations, we hyperlinked to everything we can. And, um, I think that's about it, Sam.

Dr. Sam Dubé: Yeah. Well, thanks to you. And, uh, Robert F. Kennedy Jr. for your tireless work. And I know you've had personal experience in this area and for that I'm very sorry. And, uh, hopefully we can, um, speak again. I'd really love to speak with you again.

Mary Holland: I would love to do that. I apologize that it wasn't open longer for today, but I'd be delighted to come back.

Dr. Sam Dubé: No, we're very grateful. You've taken the time out of your very busy schedule. I can only imagine what things are like now for CHD. So it's, childrenshealthdefense.org. And I'm going to put that in the description on behalf of myself, Dr. Sam Dubé, and the *Toronto Business Journal*. I want to thank you, Mary Holland Esquire, for joining us today and sharing us, not only your insights, but your professional, uh, expertise. So once again, thank you and Godspeed, Mary.

Mary Holland: Godspeed.

APPENDIX 4

Dr. Roger Hodkinson—The Oppression of Medical Science and Truth

Dr. Sam Dubé: HELLO, Dr. Sam Dubé here once again for the *Toronto Business Journal*. And I am joined here today by, uh, none other than Dr. Roger Hodkinson. Now, we've had some esteemed guests on our show, including Dr. Pierre Kory and Dr. Peter McCullough. And, uh, I think it's very fair to say that, uh, Dr. Roger Hodkinson is probably the most well-rounded and most experienced physician speaking to the issue of the pandemic in the world today. Uh, Dr. Hodkinson has... First, he's insisted that I call him Roger and, uh, and I'm honoured, uh, Roger, and please call me Sam obviously.

Dr. Roger Hodkinson: Sam, I said, unless you want to annoy me.

Dr. Sam Dubé: That's right. You did say that. I don't want to annoy you. I think there may be a Hulk in there somewhere inside, and we're seeing some of that now, actually, with you taking the gloves off. But, uh, you've lived your life, your, your,

your professional life, literally on the edge of clinical medicine. And, uh, currently you are chairman of a biotech company that is involved in DNA sequencing for cancer, and we'll leave it at that. And, uh, it is an honour to speak to you, sir. Now, just in saying, I think I have heard you speak when I was in medical school. And I mentioned that to you and it may have had to do with smoking cessation. But I do remember very clearly recognizing your voice when one night I was surfing the web looking for pandemic information and I came across the Zoom call that was posted of you, audio only, on a small town hall meeting, uh, in Alberta, where you basically said that we were being led down the garden path by our officers of health, if I recall with our previous conversation.

Dr. Roger Hodkinson: That's exactly what I said.

Dr. Sam Dubé: Yes. And, uh, and you know, I listened to you very carefully. And, uh, and it was very clear, uh, who was speaking at that point and with what authority. And I remember the reaction of that town hall, um, committee. And what was very interesting and I'll shut up in a moment, was within days the "fact-checkers," the only thing they could do was express that, "We don't know if this was Roger Hodgkinson speaking. We know it was a voice, someone claiming to be him." And then shortly after that, they misquoted one of your credentials. They misquoted you completely from that town hall Zoom audio and then addressed the Royal College based on that misquote, whereupon they claim that they had never heard of anyone in that position. Of course, they hadn't. They made up the title either, you know, it was by accident or on purpose. So, could you speak a little bit to that town hall meeting and, uh, to the subsequent fallout? And then I remember you did appear in person after that uh, and you spoke and made it very clear that you were, who you were.

Dr. Roger Hodkinson: Well, it was back in November last year. The madness has been going on for quite a while. Um, the council was considering what they called an "extension of the mask mandate." And, um, I felt I had to stand up. As I lived in Edmonton, I felt I had to stand up and be counted. Uh, what I didn't realize is that I wasn't standing up to be counted. I had to sit down for a whole day to be counted, to get my five minutes in. My office staff were hanging on the line. And, um, I'd simply written down a bunch of chicken scratch that I read from where my five minutes came up and never dreaming of course that it would get the attention that it did. Um, that was not my intent. Um, I just wanted to try and set a few things straight locally. Um, but I, you know, I was brought up in Manchester, and, um, I support Manchester United. And we have a horrible reputation for speaking our mind. So, I think that's what got me into trouble.

Dr. Sam Dubé: Well, um, you know, I was familiar with some of your credentials, and we had put them up on the screen here earlier. Um, but I wanted to summarize, uh, that with, uh, your vast experience and your well-rounded approach. Um, you know, it was very interesting again, how they tried to discredit you. But let's move on to something of more importance. So, in the past, you have stated that the real telltale sign that there's something terribly wrong in this declaration of emergency. Uh, and yet this contradiction where you must take the vaccines that are essentially...there was a shortcut taken to get them allowed. They were never approved. Um, there's questionable safety, uh, and we can go even further.

Dr. Roger Hodkinson: Not questionable safety. Totally unsafe at this point.

Dr. Sam Dubé: It's totally unsafe. And yet, established, decades-old Nobel prize, winning safe and cheap medication that can be repurposed was suppressed. Um, Dr. Peter McCullough called it, I think he called it early treatment nihilism. Is that the term that he used? He coined. And, uh, misinformation even spread about, uh, in particular hydroxychloroquine and ivermectin. And, in fact, a study just came out. What was it, two days ago? Again, absolutely promoting the, uh, benefits, uh, utility and, uh, safety of ivermectin.

Dr. Roger Hodkinson: That was by Tess Lawrie who has an exceptional meta-analysis of all the publications done to date.

Dr. Sam Dubé: And, uh, you know, it's very clear that, uh, there are some things that are terribly, terribly wrong here. And, uh, I will leave it to you now to pick it up from there, Roger.

Dr. Roger Hodkinson: Well, yes, you started out beautifully. I do appreciate that, Sam. Um, they can't have it both ways. They can't say out of one side of the mouth, this is an emergency, which it's not by the way. But even if you accept that it is an emergency with an emergency authorization for an unsafe vaccine, if you're saying that out of one side of your mouth.

Then you can't say out of the other side of your mouth, we're going to totally prohibit physicians from prescribing medications that could well be very helpful if not curative, um, for many people that actually come down with COVID. You can't have it both ways. And they want it both ways. The motivation for that of course is a bit sinister. But, um, you know, essentially what we're saying to people who think they've got COVID and go to the hospital with the right symptoms and the test comes back positive for COVID, it could be a false positive, of course, it could be the flu. Um, but we're saying to them, "Look, uh, your oxygen level. It really isn't that bad, you know? Um, we're just going to send you home." Uh, the subtext of that is, *"Come back when you're blue, when you're really desperate without any medication whatsoever that is available, that could well be a lifesaver for you. But just go home and come back when you're blue."* That's what we're saying to people in emergency departments. It's absolutely outrageous.

Dr. Sam Dubé: And we know what was happening to people once they were admitted to emergency departments and then ICUs and put on ventilators, which turned out to not be the best approach, blowing out people's alveoli. They should have been put on supplemental oxygen. But more than that, uh, they should have been recommended a certain treatment.

Dr. Roger Hodkinson: That is medical malpractice: to deny someone a therapy that is known to be probably effective. You know, as you know, in medicine, Sam, um, most drugs don't work in most people. Right. Um, no drug is guaranteed to be a hundred percent successful. That's why, when we're giving patients that piece of paper called a prescription, we say two words that we understand, that we understand and they don't. The two words are, "try this." Right? So, denying people access to a medication or two medications or three, including vitamin D, that could well be life-saving: that is medical malpractice. And we will explore the other areas of medical malpractice. As we go along. This whole episode is replete with profound medical malpractice. And that's just one example.

Dr. Sam Dubé: It's just one example. And like you said, we're going to get to that. But there is one major issue that you wanted to address. We spoke, uh, over the phone, uh, at length, and, uh, you were very, uh, intent on getting this out there. And that is the issue of, uh, the experimental gene therapy, injections, or "vaccines" in children. Um, Roger, could you please address this for us?

Dr. Roger Hodkinson: It's utter madness. It's state-sanctioned child abuse. Period. Children are not dying of this condition. In fact, over all of North America, there isn't a single reported case of a child dying of COVID who did not already have a very serious underlying disease. And if they do get COVID, even assuming the test is correct, which of course the vast majority of the time, it's not. And we'll talk about that too. Um, they're not going to... they don't have a severe disease. It's frivolous. It's like a cold. They brush it off.

So, if children are not dying of this condition, and by the way, more children die of influenza every year. Children are not dying at the same number as they do with influenza. So, if they're not suffering from this in any way whatsoever, why in God's name, would you subject them to a highly experimental, unsafe vaccine that has, as we are starting to discover, unfortunately, uh, should have been done during a clinical trial that normally extends over five to seven years. But we're finding now after the fact with the biggest uncontrolled experiments in medical history, that all kinds of adverse effects of a serious nature are coming out of the woodwork and also the risk, potential risk, not proven, of infertility involving males and females. So, why would you do that to children? And why would you entice them and shame them and then encourage them to take it with, you know, free ice-cream

Dr. Sam Dubé: Yeah, exactly. Like in Toronto.

Dr. Roger Hodkinson: Why would you do that? It's a trivial thing for kids. They're not giving it to teachers. They're not infectious. That's being shown to be clear. Um, why would you then turn around and inject them with a substance that is experimental and has a growing number of serious side effects such as myocarditis recently being discussed? And, as you know, that's the subject of an emergency meeting for the CDC that has been postponed very conveniently. Meanwhile, kids are being vaccinated. Hello?

Dr. Sam Dubé: Yep.

Dr. Roger Hodkinson: That's unacceptable. For some bureaucratic reason to delay an emergency meeting when young men and boys are coming down with myocarditis in relatively large numbers. Totally unacceptable.

Dr. Sam Dubé: And, as we both know, and you better than me, myocarditis, the damaging effects of that can manifest much later in life. Years, even decades later.

Dr. Roger Hodkinson: Yes, you and I certainly know a lot about that, but for the lay public who are listening to this, let me explain how significant this is. Myocarditis is the word we use for inflammation of the heart, the main pump that sustains life. And if there's inflammation of the heart, then there's random death of individual cells in that pump that make the pump work. And there's no way of knowing the percentage of that cell death. You just have to guess from the severity of the chest pain and the shortness of breath and how fast the heart is beating, et cetera. But it's well known, before COVID, that myocarditis, you may appear to recover from it, and then 20 years later, you come down with unexplained, premature heart failure because the reserve of the heart, if you like, has been destroyed and only becomes apparent when you lose additional reserve because you're getting older. So, CDC is calling that "mild" and the other word they use is "imbalanced."

Well, you're damned right, it's imbalanced. It's the CDC that's imbalanced here. Myocarditis is never mild, especially in young men. No, it's not. That's a contortion of the English language. Again, we're seeing words were used inappropriately throughout this entire episode. We'll talk about cases, which they're not, of course, um, yeah. "Safety, cases, mild." You see them morphing the language to fit the narrative all the time, otherwise known as a bold-faced lie.

Dr. Sam Dubé: You know, we're seeing, uh, young men, uh, athletes, um, crippled, we're seeing cases among, uh, young women as well. Um, parents are feeling pressure, social pressure... not knowing who to trust. I mean, what more pain could there be than that of an anguished mother who convinced her son who didn't want to get the vaccine, right, and we've seen this, uh, go and get it and now he can no longer be physically active?

Dr. Roger Hodkinson: It's unconscionable. But could I, before we finish the segment on children, Sam, could I elaborate on the infertility issue?

Dr. Sam Dubé: Actually, that's what I wanted to see into next. So, you were talking about the long-term effects of myocarditis. There is another aspect here that can have terrible long-term effects, in fact, generational effects. And that is the potential for infertility. Now, I saw you on *The High Wire* a couple of days ago with Del Bigtree and it was great. It was great. And you talk to this a little bit about the, uh, expression of the ACE-2 receptors in, uh, testicles and in the small intestine and I believe in ovaries as well. And, uh, in the uterus. Is that, uh, correct?

Dr. Roger Hodkinson: Not the ovaries so much. Um, we'll differentiate male and female here. It's quite important to understand the difference…

Dr. Sam Dubé: Please

Dr. Roger Hodkinson: …In why there's a potential. I underlined it in neon. I'm not a scaremonger. I'm simply referring to the medical literature and talking about caution. And show me I'm wrong. That's what I'm talking about. Because fertility is something very, very significant. Um, and it can't be just brushed away under the guise of a rushed, reckless, um, introduction of an experimental vaccine. With respect to girls, let's deal with them first.

Dr. Sam Dubé: Please.

Dr. Roger Hodkinson: First of all, you and I know, but the general public does not know, that a baby girl is born with all her eggs in her ovaries. That's it. They don't make more of them. If they die, they're done.

Dr. Sam Dubé: Full complement for the rest of her life.

Dr. Roger Hodkinson: That's right. That's right. They're very precious cargo. Right there at birth. Um, now it just so happens that the, uh, Pfizer's submission to the Japanese authorities has just been translated. And it's clear that in the what's called biodistribution study, that means trying to figure out where these little particles in the vaccine go in the body. Where do they locate? A very important part of any medication, um, study, particularly with vaccines. And then particularly of course, with new technology like this. Um, now this study was in rats, uh, not humans, um, for obvious reasons. And they found that much to everyone's surprise these particles were located heavily in the ovaries. That was it. No further studies, no other animal studies, different types of animals, which they're obligated to do. All that we know at this point in time, is that in rats, these vaccine particles heavily aggregate in the ovaries. Now that's a huge alarm bell because we don't know what the consequences of that is.

Dr. Sam Dubé: No.

Dr. Roger Hodkinson: It may be nothing, but show me that it's not. Because when we're dealing with infertility, you cannot check for that in a trial that runs four to six months. The last time I checked, um, Sam, correct me if I'm wrong here, but in medical school, weren't we taught that, um, pregnancy lasts nine months. Is that correct?

Dr. Sam Dubé: In humans? Yes. Yes. That's about average. Yes. Nine months is the figure they gave us.

Dr. Roger Hodkinson: How can you possibly check for infertility if you do a trial for four to six months?

Dr. Sam Dubé: You can't.

Dr. Roger Hodkinson: With males, it's a different story. Um, this isn't experimental data, as you know. This is published data before COVID. Um, let me just sidetrack here a little bit into how this vaccine works. Um, the vaccine is intended to produce, um, a particular protein from the virus. It's called the spike protein. And the production of that spike protein is then, it's intended that the immune system reacts to that to produce the long-term immunity to the virus itself. Now, it just so happens that the spike protein, uh, has a specific receptor in the body. It's called the A-C-E 2 receptor, A-C-E 2 receptor. It's very widely distributed, and that's how it gets into the body in the first place: through the back of the throat and the upper respiratory tract.

But that receptor is very widely expressed in the body. It's on the inside surface of every blood vessel, arteries, capillaries, and veins throughout the entire body, the brain included, the endometrium included, we'll come to that, the lining of the uterus. And we believe that it's the attachment of the spike protein to that very specific receptor that starts the clotting process inside the blood vessel, obstructing the blood vessel and causing problems in the distribution of that blood vessel. Now, two of the organs in the body that have the highest expression of the A-C-E 2 receptor are the placenta. Does that get your attention?

Dr. Sam Dubé: Yeah, the most fragile tissue in the human body, right?

Dr. Roger Hodkinson: In addition to the endometrium. Mm, that's the placenta and the testis, unexpectedly. The testis has a very high concentration. Um, and in fact, it was shown, uh, with autopsies on people who've died of the infection itself, that there was inflammation in the testes in some of these people. We call it orchitis, medically, in fact. Inflammation of the testes. So, if the testes are a focus of attack of the spike protein, again, we don't know what that translates into. Um, oh, I'm sorry that the previous study. It wasn't an autopsy. I beg your pardon. It was men who had had COVID, the infection.

Dr. Sam Dubé: Yes

Dr. Roger Hodkinson: And this is coming out of Israel. Now it was shown that they had reduced sperm count.

Dr. Sam Dubé: Right.

Dr. Roger Hodkinson: So, there's good reason to be worried about if the spike protein attaches to the same receptors, could the same result happen?

Dr. Sam Dubé: And this is in addition to, you've expressed concern, as have many other experts, about the reduced sperm count over the last few decades in general.

Dr. Roger Hodkinson: Yes, that would compound the unexplained reduction, about 40% reduction in sperm counts internationally, that we really don't know the cause of. We don't need another hit on male fertility, obviously. And yet, despite that potential underlined unproven, despite that potential risk, we are currently injecting millions of young men with this experimental vaccine, not knowing anything about its possible consequences on fertility. I want to be wrong.

Dr. Sam Dubé: Yes.

Dr. Roger Hodkinson: I'm not a scaremonger. All I'm saying is that prudent traditional medicine, being very risk-averse should be saying "stop the train," not just for myocarditis reasons, but for the fact that the ominous potential of infertility for different reasons in girls and boys.

Dr. Sam Dubé: Yep. And it should be said you're not a conspiracy theorist. You're not an anti-vaxxer. You're not a "Great Resetter."

Dr. Roger Hodkinson: Not at all.

Dr. Sam Dubé: You're approaching this as the quintessential physician, "do no harm," with decades of experience in a variety of different subspecialties, in a variety of different areas, and your alarm bells are just going off like crazy.

Dr. Roger Hodkinson: Yes, the two central ethics in medicine that you and I were taught in medical school. First, do no harm, and informed consent. They're both being massively abrogated. First, do no harm, of course, with the lockdowns, which are causing massive harm, in many, many areas as we're well aware of now. Um, but also the potential for harm, with fertility and myocarditis and whatever. You know, it's the old story, you don't know what you don't know. That's the whole reason for clinical trials. If we knew what could happen, we wouldn't need a clinical trial. We're doing it to look for the unexpected and to quantify it and to determine how relevant it is relative to the benefit. We don't know. And the second ethic is even more important in many respects. And that is informed consent. Because when you see the billboards while driving home, encouraging everyone to, you know, pull together and get vaccinated. "It's safe." You know? You don't want to be responsible for granny dying. Do you? You know? All that inducement that's going on is very sinister. Um, that's a very important medical ethic.

Dr. Sam Dubé: Coercion. The word is coercion.

Dr. Roger Hodkinson: And the colleges, of course. Um, the colleges that are suppressing physicians brutally across this country. Their principal reason for existence, I could describe as to protect the lay public from you and me. Right? It's to make sure we're not cutting off the wrong leg. It's to make sure that we're not pedophiles and doing all those good things on behalf of the general public. But what are the colleges doing now? They're supposed to be the guardians of the public against medical malpractice. Instead of that, they are themselves guilty of medical malpractice because of all the evidence of the harm that's going on and the lack of informed consent that's going on. And yet, despite knowing that and therefore guilty of medical malpractice; despite knowing that, and their normal function would be to blow the whistle and say, "stop." They're not banging the desk of the medical officers of health across this country to say, "Why are you doing this? It's hurting people. You shouldn't be doing this. You should stop right now," just as they would talk to you and me. Right?

Dr. Sam Dubé: Right.

Dr. Roger Hodkinson: Treating your patient. So, this is so Orwellian. Everything is upside down in this story. Everything is the opposite of what it should be. Truth has gone out of the window. Colleges of physicians are practicing medical malpractice. How Orwellian is that?

Dr. Sam Dubé: And just like the CPSO, when was it? April 30th issued a letter threatening, uh, physicians in Ontario, uh, to basically keep your mouth shut about any other alternative therapies, uh, towing the company line. And there was an outcry. There was an outcry. As the NDMP, uh, Derek Sloan, uh, announced a couple of days ago, he's been getting hundreds of emails from physicians and healthcare workers over this. And like, what is going on here? What is going on? And like you said, it's in direct contravention to their decree to protect people, the public.

Dr. Roger Hodkinson: The messenger, as they call it, a somewhat, um, unfortunate term. The messenger that comes out, the letter that goes to every physician in Alberta actually said "Listen." Essentially what they said was this, *"We're listening. We're watching. Be careful of what you say. Whatever you say has to be based on fact and not hearsay."* Well, there's another Orwellian twist, isn't it? Because the facts that they claim are nothing of the sort. They're all arbitrary measures dreamt up by politicians to save their skin, nothing more, nothing less.

Dr. Sam Dubé: Right. And one in particular, as we've discussed before you and I, and that is flip-flop Fauci.

Dr. Roger Hodkinson: Let me continue.

Dr. Sam Dubé: We can address that later.

Dr. Roger Hodkinson: Let me continue with that particular edition of the messenger because it wasn't just warning physicians to be very careful and, you know, people do snitch on you, you know? Oh no, they went beyond that. They went beyond that. That wasn't enough. They were warning us, "Be very careful of what you say to your neighbors." That was in print.

Dr. Sam Dubé: Really? I wasn't aware of that at all. Oh, my goodness. Oh, my goodness.

Dr. Roger Hodkinson: Again, Orwellian.

Dr. Sam Dubé: What is going on?

Dr. Roger Hodkinson: Because as you and I know, they have the opportunity to deny you a livelihood like that

Dr. Sam Dubé: Like that. Yeah. And there are physicians who are putting their necks out. Uh, one, uh, um, Patrick Phillips, a family doctor.

Dr. Roger Hodkinson: Very brave

Dr. Sam Dubé: Unbelievable, unbelievable. He couldn›t take it anymore. He knew he… "I couldn›t live with myself anymore without doing anything. I had to say something given what I was seeing with my patients."

Dr. Roger Hodkinson: If you're knowledgeable and you're silent, you are culpable in the consequences. Because when we get that precious title, doctor, it implies great ethical training, it implies that you care, that you put society before yourself at all times. He's very brave. He's very brave

Dr. Sam Dubé: Boy, oh boy. We need others to follow suit. You know? Um, there are so many things I want to speak to you about. Um, can we move on from, uh, children? And, uh, I did want to mention something a little bit more about, uh, pregnant women and how I mean, there were none involved in the initial. Right?

Dr. Roger Hodkinson: No, they were specifically excluded along with children and old people and immunocompromised people. They just chose to experiment on the working well. The only pregnancy, uh, trial you might say was the 40 or so women who got unintentionally pregnant during the trial. And that was it. An insignificant number.

Dr. Sam Dubé: And, uh, now we're seeing yellow card, uh, recordings in Britain and VAERS reports of not only, um, as we were discussing before, uh, abnormal menstruation, um, and post-menopausal women, uh, experiencing bleeding, but miscarriages,

Dr. Roger Hodkinson: Yes. Let, let me talk as a pathologist now.

Dr. Sam Dubé: Please

Dr. Roger Hodkinson: About pregnancy. Even gynecologists don›t see what we see. When we get a uterus in the lab, we open it up and we actually see the endometrium, the lining of the uterus under direct vision. There it is in front of us. We're cutting into it. The endometrium is the most fragile, lush, tissue in the entire human body. It's intended to be so because that's the destination for a fertilized egg that wants to implant in a luxurious environment to grow the initial cell stage. It's intended to be so. And the blood vessels in the endometrium under the microscope are the most fragile in the human body. Incredibly fine um, anastomotic, sinusoids. Lakes of blood vessels. And it takes very, very little to block one of those vessels off with a blood clot. And so, you can see where I'm going with this.

Dr. Sam Dubé: Yes

Dr. Roger Hodkinson: The endometrium, the lining of the uterus, has blood vessels like everywhere else. That's why women bleed every month. And just imagine for a moment, you've got a fertilized egg coming down the fallopian tube. You've got an egg coming down the fallopian tube, it gets fertilized, right? And it lands on the endometrium and it's supposed to grow and be very comfortable there. Um, so what happens if along comes a big bolus of spike protein and starts attacking the blood vessels? Boom. You're done.

And the woman might not even know about it if it's very, very early on in pregnancy, but it could be the reason why we're seeing these first trimester miscarriages. Again, we don't know. It's not being studied. We don't know the frequency of it. Spontaneous abortions happen all the time. Is it the background frequency or is this something extra on top of that? We don't know. Isn't that tragic to say? Something as fundamental as that. We don't know what impact this so-called vaccine has on the viability of early pregnancies.

Dr. Sam Dubé: I wanted to ask you also about, uh, another aspect, uh, another mechanism, and that is with the. uh, similar to the spike protein and the potential for developing antibodies against your own placental tissue. Is that a potential or real…?

Dr. Roger Hodkinson: It was an initial concern. I think it's been put to rest. I don't think there's much cross-reactivity here that was originally thought of as possible. But I think that's been excluded now, uh, as pathogenesis, as we say that link to the effect. It's much more likely that that's based upon the A-C-E 2 receptor in the endometrium and the excess of the spike protein. Because you see, um, again, I'm talking to the choir here.

Dr. Sam Dubé: Well, you're talking to everybody, I'm just the facilitator.

Dr. Roger Hodkinson: Let me explain for the general public. Just about every biological function follows what we call a bell curve. Some people do more of something than others and some people do less. It's just a standard part of physiology. And what's probably happening here, again, we don't know, but the reasonable supposition is that some people who couldn't be identified before they get the jab, some people are at the extreme end of that curve and they produce a huge amount of spike protein as opposed to the bulk of people in the middle that don't. And it's those people, I suspect. It's just my theory. I've got no reason to support this. Again, the studies have not been done. But I would strongly suspect that the people that are getting into trouble with

thromboses and lost pregnancies, um, are people who unexpectedly produce an over-abundance of the spike protein. And they're
the ones that are getting into trouble.

Dr. Sam Dubé: Again, common sense, you know, um, the bell
curve, the distribution. And we don't know because these studies
were never done. So, it seems like there was some gross negli-
gence, uh, involved in the formation preparation...

Dr. Roger Hodkinson: You know what? In medicine, Sam, we
don't have a word for how gross this is. I mean, this is over the top.

Dr. Sam Dubé: It is

Dr. Roger Hodkinson: Never seen anything close to this scale.

Dr. Sam Dubé: And, you know, um, there are so many directions.
I want to go with this, but if we look, at okay, now studies are
starting to be done after the fact to quote you. After the fact. And
we're starting to see some very scary results. Just even observa-
tionally, like with myocarditis, the much, you know, increased
prevalence of that. But when we're looking at the spike protein
itself, and Dr. Byram Bridle, for instance, uh, sounded an alarm
a couple of weeks ago on the Alex Pierson show. It was, I think,
an eight-minute sequence. It was gone three days later. And he
basically said the two big assumptions, uh, predicated on the
vaccines that they were safe, was well, the mRNA and the spike
protein stay in one place. They don't migrate from the deltoid.
They stay near the injection site. They don't accumulate anywhere.
And the second one...

Dr. Roger Hodkinson: That's not true.

Dr. Roger Hodkinson Dr. Sam Dubé: Exactly. The two big ones: that, and that the spike protein was completely safe. These are both totally wrong. He said, "We made a terrible mistake."

Dr. Roger Hodkinson: Right? Well, but even that. I mean, in fairness to him, I admire his bravery, and a lot of what he said was dead right. But, I mean, the whole purpose of injecting it into the deltoid muscle is a safe place to put it. You know, you're not making anything there. There are no cells to pick it up, to process it, to create a reaction.

Dr. Sam Dubé: So, they already knew

Dr. Roger Hodkinson: It goes up to the endolymphaticus, up to the axilla where the lymphoid tissue is, and it's mopped up there by these two cells that are intended to pick it up and then react to it. Um, that gets a bit technical. And I suspect that it's the inability in some people to mop up all that spike protein that's being produced in your armpit. It gets into the general circulation and creates all these thrombotic problems. But, you know, we don't… There's not a reaction to the vaccine in the muscle. It's um, it's all a matter of the lymphoid system.

Dr. Sam Dubé: That's right. And he was saying how this is new. This is not new. This is not new. This has been known for quite some time. But he did say we've made a terrible mistake.

Dr. Roger Hodkinson: Huge

Dr. Sam Dubé: Yes. And then, uh….

Dr. Roger Hodkinson: Just to digress, Jay Bhattacharya said, out of Stanford, one of the most esteemed epidemiologists in the whole world, who said exactly that with reference to lockdowns:

"This is the biggest mistake we've made in public health ever." Sorry, I digress, but…

Dr. Sam Dubé: No, I mean, we want to address this Roger, for sure.

Dr. Roger Hodkinson: That was a similar statement.

Dr. Sam Dubé: And I›m familiar with, uh, Dr. Bhattacharya. I believe he›s also an economist, uh, and you know, in addition to being a medical doctor and, uh, he was also uh, a consultant to, uh, governor DeSantis, I believe on the lockdowns in Florida. Yeah. And look at Florida now, you know. Look at them. They're thriving.

Dr. Roger Hodkinson: The same demographics, the same scary variants. Exactly the same as we're facing in Canada and two diametrically opposite reactions.

Dr. Sam Dubé: Unbelievable. So, let's take a look at that. Let's take a look at this early mismanagement. First of all, let's take a look at the testing, the PCR testing.

Dr. Roger Hodkinson: Could we get one step further down the rabbit hole perhaps before we…

Dr. Sam Dubé: Absolutely.

Dr. Roger Hodkinson: So. Flip-flop Fauci wanted to do this bizarre thing called "gain-of-function" research, which means making a virus more infectious in order to study it better. Bizarre as that seems, he wanted that done. Obama had said, "Not on my watch, I'm prohibiting it." And so, he intentionally bypassed that prohibition in the States, through a white-gloved intermediary that might camouflage the trail who then subcontracted it to this lab in Wuhan.

Dr. Sam Dubé: You're talking about Dr. Daszak and the Equal Health Alliance.

Dr. Roger Hodkinson: Exactly. Now that lab was known to have terrible biosafety. It was the reason for state department communiqués well before COVID.

Dr. Sam Dubé: Yes. And that was reported. Yeah.

Dr. Roger Hodkinson: And he still sends it there. They're very knowledgeable about the fact that that has very poor biosafety. So yeah, they did all their work there and they genetically engineered this thing. And you know, no lab, even in the States, can be 100.000% safe because it's got things called people working in there. And you can't control the human element. And lo and behold, predictably, this genetically engineered virus. Not intentionally I'm sure, because it's a lousy bioterrorism weapon. It doesn't kill enough people.

It got out into the local environment, got on planes to be on land faster than you could spit because of the demands of the Italian leather industry. And a lot of them came from Wuhan, got going into the local environment. Um, Milan still has the largest concentration of elderly people in nursing homes in the whole of Europe. And so it was, um, a perfect storm. They started dying in large numbers. Then, I've got to be careful with the laws of slander here.

Dr. Sam Dubé: Okay.

Dr. Roger Hodkinson: One Neil Ferguson at Imperial College, London, got ahold of those numbers and plugged them into his computer programming with artificial intelligence and all kinds of assumptions, and pronounced to the entire world that Armageddon was coming.

Dr. Sam Dubé: Yes.

Dr. Roger Hodkinson: He'd been wrong serially with previous epidemics.

Dr. Sam Dubé: Yes.

Dr. Roger Hodkinson: And so the first big mistake other than Fauci starting it off, the first really big mistake was that no one internationally did due diligence on Ferguson, knowing full well how notoriously wrong he had been. Everyone accepted those numbers at face value. And then the rest is history. They all started introducing these mandates to protect.

Dr. Sam Dubé: Based on those figures.

Dr. Roger Hodkinson: Because, you know, "We are your big protector and we will protect you from everything from cradle to grave." And this is merely one example. So that's really how this whole thing started. Um, and I can't remember how I digressed into that.

Dr. Sam Dubé: No, no, no. And that's fine because we were going to talk about the PCR testing, but this is better. I'm really glad because I wasn't sure if you wanted to speak to the origin. But didn't Fauci also, I mean, he basically perjured himself in front of Senator. Dr. Wrenn Paul. He didn't even know what the definition of "gain-of-function" was, allegedly. And to be clear....

Dr. Roger Hodkinson: Oh, no. Oh no, no, no. He knows more about "gain-of-function" than anyone living.

Dr. Sam Dubé: Sure.

Dr. Roger Hodkinson: Um, he is a vile man. He knows exactly.... That was a heavily lawyered response. He knew exactly that he was the bunny in the headlights. He's the walking dead right now. Uh, he can't survive that. Okay. PCR. So, this whole thing gets going.

Dr. Sam Dubé: Why did they decide on using the PCR test when Kary Mullis, who invented that test–he died in 2019, allegedly before COVID–stated, "You can't use my test to diagnose any kind of illness?" And you go beyond what, how many amplifications? About 30 amplifications. And you basically can amplify anything that you find and make it something to talk about right? Even less.

Dr. Roger Hodkinson: 25 should be the max. Um, yeah, so, you know, this whole concept of testing people who feel perfectly well to see if they have a strand, literally a strand of virus, in their nose is ridiculous medically. Who cares? It's irrelevant. What really matters is, are you infectious? Do you have a clinical infection? And it was even more ridiculous because they were prohibiting treating it in the first place. So, why are you bothering to find out? It just so happens that the test is so lousy. And I happen to know a fair bit about this for the reasons why. The test is so lousy, that when you test totally well people and you crank up the number of times you multiply what you've got, the so-called cycle times for PCR, by the time you get up to 40 cycles, you get almost a hundred percent positives, false positives. And the true positivity range of people who are actually infectious, who have enough virus in their nose to spread it to someone else, is extremely small.

And so, it was totally inappropriate technology used in the wrong way. Whereas in normal times, what would happen is you present to a hospital if you're sick, and that's where a sample gets taken to be tested. And that's a much lower volume of testing than it would be to test the whole population. And at that point of care, that's when the gold standard method of identifying any bug should have been used. And that gold standard is called DNA sequencing by the Sangha method. Fred Sangha got the Nobel prize for it. Well-known technology. Anyone that says that PCR is the gold standard, again, it's a monstrous lie. Anyone in the game knows that it's a terrible technology. Um, and they could have easily scaled up DNA sequencing by the traditional method to be tested centrally with a much-reduced volume than would be needed and gather verifiably accurate results. They chose not to do that.

Dr. Sam Dubé: Why, Roger?

Dr. Roger Hodkinson: Well, the machines were out there. The PCR machines. The company selling them was pushing them like crazy. It was immediately available. Um, the fact that it's cranking out false positives would have been…they weren't ignorant of that. Oh no. Oh no. It served to drive the fear when you see those graphs in the morning paper. What a beautiful vehicle it is to intimidate people into action? Because those graphs should be cut down by 95%. And suddenly you've got a little blip. You don't have a big curve, right? Um, no, they've known this all along. It's just being dragged out of them in court. You know, the whole… Manitoba, for example, um, in the court case that recently went on. It was dragged out of the provincial laboratory there that they knew that anything over 25 cycles or so, um, you know, they knew that that was a false positive. Um, that they were only getting growth, uh, culture, positive results at 25 cycles.

They've known that. They've known that from the get-go. And yet the explanation for that was pathetic. The explanation was, "Well, we're only doing that because we don't want to miss a single case." Well, of course, you won't, you idiots. You won't miss a single case. I can guarantee that, but you'll get 99% false positives for God's sake. Listen, let me draw an analogy here. I used to inspect laboratories for the very college that's got its teeth in me. And I had the power to shut down the lab. Now, if I had walked into a lab and I looked at the books and I saw that 70% of pap smears were being called cancer, shut down.

Dr. Sam Dubé: Shut down.

Dr. Roger Hodkinson: Right there that afternoon. You're not going to read a single one until you can figure out what's going wrong here. What's the difference? Pap smears are a screening test for cervical cancer in females. It's not very common. And if I oversaw a lab that was reporting 70% as positive, obviously falsely positive, that lab would be shut down immediately, on the spot. What's the difference now? people are walking around feeling perfectly well who being called positive for COVID. 95 or more percent of the time, dead wrong.

Dr. Sam Dubé: Counted as a case.

Dr. Roger Hodkinson: But it gets much worse than that because then their contacts have to be traced and whatever the false positive rate is, you multiply by 10. And then a whole team of people is taken out of the workforce. The idiocy of this from a medical perspective is indescribable. It's a nightmare of stupidity.

Dr. Sam Dubé: Grossly overinflated case counts.

Dr. Roger Hodkinson: And that was one of the things that maintained fear. The other thing, of course, that maintains fear is the absence of any counter-narrative that's driving the fear. So, when politicians and the media and physicians, the three usual sources of information, when they're uniformly and brutally suppressed, the average individual who feels in their gut that this doesn't make sense. There's no way of confirming that.

Dr. Sam Dubé: No.

Dr. Roger Hodkinson: And those are the two drivers: the PCR madness, the so-called PCR-demic

Dr. Sam Dubé: And no counter-narrative.

Dr. Roger Hodkinson: And no counter-narrative. And so, the lay public is walking around with these diapers on their faces for absolutely no reason.

Dr. Sam Dubé: Well, let's talk about the masking.

Dr. Roger Hodkinson: Masks don't work. Social distancing doesn't work.

Dr. Sam Dubé: Masking didn't work for the flu, right? Masking doesn't work for the flu. And then all of a sudden, "Wow. It works for…:

Dr. Roger Hodkinson: If we found the magic for controlling the flu with sophisticated medicine, don't you think we would have used it? We didn't use it because it doesn't exist. You cannot control a nanoscale problem with a macro-scale solution, a mask. It's intuitive nonsense. And then, of course, there was the Danish study, the best controlled study on masks that nailed that coffin shut. Because at the end of the day, there are only two reasons to wear masks. One is to stop me from giving it to you. And the other is to stop you from giving it to me. Well, if I have it, guess what happened with the flu? I didn't need a test. I didn't need a mask. I stayed home. I had chicken noodle soup. I sprinkled it with Tylenol. I went to bed. I sweated it out. I'd need no testing of any kind, no involvement with the government. And when I decided personally to feel good enough to go back to work, I went back to work and it worked beautifully. Because along the way, someone brought me the chicken noodle soup and they got it too, not intentionally, but we all knew it happened. That's called building herd immunity, the natural way, the safe way. With the whole virus, not just a bit of it. Better immunity, safer method, instantly available and at no cost. That's how we handled the flu. And this time it should be absolutely no different. So, masks don't work. Social distancing doesn't work because of the aerosol that's created.

Dr. Sam Dubé: Aerosolization.

Dr. Roger Hodkinson: Which travels a long distance. It's in every aisle in Walmart, whether there's someone there or not. So, you're subjected to one of, what I may call the risks of everyday life. You don't know if you're going to have a stroke tomorrow. You don't know if you're going to have a head-on collision on the road going home, and you don't know what you're breathing in the aisle at Walmart. Welcome to life. It's a risk of living. And government cannot and should not try to protect you from everything. That's social distancing. Travel bans by the same token. If masks and social distancing don't work, obviously travel bans don't, uh, either. I'm sorry, uh, aircraft travel. Um, travel bans, so far as

Canada's concerned, we're the poorest border with thousands of truck drivers coming in every day that aren't tested. Why are we putting people in quarantine prisons?

Dr. Sam Dubé: With air travel. I know.

Dr. Roger Hodkinson: I know. Oh, come on, come on. I mean, you know. I mean, whose legs are you pulling here?

Dr. Sam Dubé: But even the twisted logic of the mask. Well, if you walk into a restaurant, you know, and your mask as soon as you sit down and you take the mask off. Oh, the virus knows not to infect anyone now, you know, because you're seated at your table. Right?

Dr. Roger Hodkinson: And who exactly decides how many people can sit at a table?

Dr. Sam Dubé: Right. Arbitrary.

Dr. Roger Hodkinson: Let me see now, should it be two and a half today or six and a quarter tomorrow? You know, the arbitrary nature of those decisions just pulled out of thin air. Um, no medical science behind it whatsoever. And then the final thing, of course, that's ludicrous is lockdowns. I mean, there've been numerous studies now showing that the scale of harm, um, vastly exceeds any trivial benefit at, you know, so many levels in society. Um, not the least of which is the tsunami of medical issues that have not been dealt with that will be hitting, you know, the healthcare system very shortly and people having died of that or having to live with an extra year of pain because you've not had your hip joint replaced. Um, you know, schools being closed and single mothers having to scramble to find daycare. Um, bankruptcies by the hundreds of thousands.

Entrepreneurs who put their life savings on the line. The very essence of capitalism. Um, and so on and so on. I mean, so, you know, what I'm saying is if you pull all those threads together–masks, social distancing, travel bans, lockdowns–and you pull it all together, you're left with one singular, take-home statement: nothing works. Nothing works. Medicine is impotent at controlling this. Get used to it. We can't control it. We have to accommodate to it as per the Great Barrington Declaration and accommodate in all the practical ways we've always done very successfully without any involvement of government and threats of experimental vaccines and so on. It's no different. With the singular exception of enhanced protection of the elderly with comorbidities.

Dr. Sam Dubé: As the declaration states, and 40,000 physicians alone, I think, signed that, and tens of thousands more researchers, and hundreds of thousands of people.

Dr. Roger Hodkinson: So, what should we do with old people? Well, first of all, they're conveniently self-quarantined already. They're in four walls and a door. And then rarely go outside. So, what we need to be doing is what's called, you know, and I know, there's a thing called an infection control manual on the shelf, getting dirty. That's how we control superbugs in hospitals. You know, established methods of preventing transmission. Well known, well documented, not being used to the extent that they should be. And then we have the additional benefit of vitamin D, which has been very well described as reducing the prevalence of COVID and severity if it happens. Um, they should all be getting vitamin D because by definition, everyone in a nursing home is vitamin D deficient. By definition because they rarely go outside to get the sun and they're not getting supplements. So, there are all kinds of things we could do to protect the elderly that we're not doing. And there's, of course also the treatment with ivermectin and hydroxichloroquine. If it was starting to show initial signs prohibited explicitly under pain of losing your livelihood, you cannot prescribe this in Canada.

Dr. Sam Dubé: Because it works. Because it is a reasonable alternative treatment, especially early treatment, because it will threaten the emergency use authorization.

Dr. Roger Hodkinson: Precisely. It's a much more effective. It's hard to quantify how many lives would have been saved with the initial use of Ivermectin. But I'm suspecting in North America, it's probably 100,000 or more unnecessary deaths, they probably wouldn't have lived that much longer. They were going to die within a couple of months anyway, but they would have had that additional few months and if you're asking someone today, do you want to live two months or not, guess what the answer is going to be?

Dr. Sam Dubé: They could have comorbidities, but they have a chance to live longer. And these are the people that are largely affected where the virus can be fatal is with the comorbidities and the vast majority the population, the viruses is at most of bad flu. You know.

Dr. Roger Hodkinson: And, you know, adults, we've been sort of accommodating and handling the stupidity all in our own ways, you know, madder than hell, but trying to accommodate. But what about those old people in the nursing homes, who for a year, had not been allowed to touch, to hug, to see their grandchildren under these tin pot idiots who are preventing that, preventing those last years of life for an elderly person, to prevent them having that intimate contact with their family. That is so despicable.

Dr. Sam Dubé: Absolutely. You know, when you're in the twilight of your life, and to have that additional constraint, system of constraints in place.

Dr. Roger Hodkinson: All for no reason, because if we had a cough and cold and we may have COVID, we didn't go to see granny in the first place.

Dr. Sam Dubé: That's right. Protect the vulnerable. That's it. Don't lock down healthy people to protect the ones that really would be affected, badly affected. And this is how we've always treated it. What's the difference?...

Dr. Roger Hodkinson: We've never quarantined the well. If we do anything, we quarantine the sick.

Dr. Sam Dubé: Yeah, unwell.

Dr. Roger Hodkinson: Never been tried before on this scale in medical history?

Dr. Sam Dubé: Now, if you want to go here, let's go here. But otherwise, if there's more you want to speak to that we've covered and you'd like to elaborate, please say so. Roger, but you spoke to me on the phone earlier about opportunism and how this virus was an opportunity. And right from the beginning, a purposeful mishandling. Can we discuss this?

Dr. Roger Hodkinson: Yes. And perhaps we could also discuss so-called shedding as well.

Dr. Sam Dubé: Oh, absolutely. Shall we talk about shedding first?

Dr. Roger Hodkinson: No, let's talk about.

Dr. Sam Dubé: The opportunism?

Dr. Roger Hodkinson: I think it's a conspiracy theory, I believe that this virus escaped simply because of sloppy biosafety in that level 4 lab in Wuhan, and it got international faster than you can split because of international air travel. It was everywhere almost immediately. And then people started sadly dying in larger numbers in nursing homes, which again is relative as you said before, with my analogy to speaking to granny, umm. Yeah, it is however, you know as they say, in American politics, never let a good crisis go to waste, and the Democrats are exceptionally good at that. Yeah, the

"Great Resetters" are taking unquestionably despicable advantage of this unexpected event that just landed in their laps. As an example of how to control the population, it's an incredible example of how fear, even if artificially created, how fear can result in control.

And that is something that taking great note of to use in other ways in the future. Suppress the media, suppress doctors, suppress politicians, and create some artificial threats that is actually quite trivial. And you've got 'em where you want them; they'll follow you because you got them scared shitless. Yeah, oh they're taking big notice of this? And it's probably one of the biggest lessons to come out of this whole mess is to be aware of how that has been manipulated. But I don't believe for a second it was planned. I mean, the thought of coordinating, you know, hundreds of countries on the same morning to do the same thing and to have them all, or part of the big lie? I don't believe that for a second. No, I think it's, it was politicians tried to play the metro game, getting caught in the unfortunate consequences of the obvious that none of this thing worked and having to double down on that, you know, like, Fauci you know, if one mess doesn't work, where to? Well, I can tell you, Dr. Fauci... ten masks would be even better, because no one would die of COVID because it all be dead of hypoxia.

Dr. Sam Dubé: Hypoxia... toxicity and maybe even asphyxiation. Well, you know, it's funny, because Fauci mentioned it, this is all on video, where he stated that he felt that the risk of doing the gain-of-function research was worth it. You know, and then denies that they ever supported or will ever support gain of function research on...

Dr. Roger Hodkinson: First off, it's such academic arrogance.

Dr. Sam Dubé: Yeah.

Dr. Roger Hodkinson: To think that to do this in isolation, and never get caught with their pants down, to think that every lab is 100% safe. I mean, that's such profound academic arrogance. And then to lie bold face about trying to nuance it the meaning of...

Dr. Sam Dubé: Uniformity.

Dr. Roger Hodkinson: Yeah, wordsmithing is, he's as guilty as hell. The most vile man walking. That's how bad it is not just starting it, but amplifying it, suppressing other treatment. He's got his sticky fingers all over this from start to finish.

Dr. Sam Dubé: And yet, the Dems are pushing for a Medal of Freedom. You heard that?

Dr. Roger Hodkinson: Well, didn't Obama get a Nobel Peace Prize after being...?

Dr. Sam Dubé: Yes, what did he do?

Dr. Roger Hodkinson: In two days or something?

Dr. Sam Dubé: Yeah, exactly now, umm. So an opportunity here that hasn't gone wasted, to exert control over our population through fear and manipulation of statistics, and suppression of free speech, especially among the qualified the people, physicians who are frontline who are concerned, trying to stick to their oath of doing no harm and informed consent to the population, neither of which are enacted. They're both violated, Nuremberg, you know, violated. And this is just going on and there's distraction after distraction after manipulation. And the CDC issued an article a few days ago, basically stating, categorically, there are no long term side effects to the vaccines and the spike protein is completely safe. Can you believe it?

Dr. Roger Hodkinson: They should be writing the horoscopes in the morning paper.

Dr. Sam Dubé: They'll be more accurate.

Dr. Roger Hodkinson: How can you possibly predict the absence of a complication until you've looked for it?

Dr. Sam Dubé: We don't know.

Dr. Roger Hodkinson: We don't know what we don't know.

Dr. Sam Dubé: Unbelievable. Now, let's speak to something that we're starting to learn something about, is that the shedding, and you mentioned on the *High Wire* as a pathologist, the concern about accumulation in the sweat glands.

Dr. Roger Hodkinson: Yeah. You know, when I first heard about this, I thought it was ridiculous.

Dr. Sam Dubé: Me too.

Dr. Roger Hodkinson: Yeah, give me a break.

Dr. Sam Dubé: I don't have your experience. But even me, I was like...

Dr. Roger Hodkinson: Yeah, I ditched it immediately. You know, it's just impossible. However, it's a grey dock that dishes 1000s of women as being subjected to group hysteria, because most of these complications are involving women with abnormal menstrual periods, and we know that the menstrual periods are significantly affected by all kinds of things, including stress. We know that, but there's so many of these complaints that dismissing them as simply group hysteria by women.

Dr. Sam Dubé: Yeah.

Dr. Roger Hodkinson: That's going to be, I think, a very humbling interpretation.

Dr. Sam Dubé: Yeah. It's gonna come out? Boy, oh boy.

Dr. Roger Hodkinson: Because there is a partial, I emphasize that there's a partial hypothesis for how this could be happening. And it's this. We know from autopsies of people who've died of COVID that the virus now, not vaccine, we know that the virus quite heavily concentrates in sweat glands. And by the way, for the information of the lay public, breasts are modified sweat glands. So there's a risk here for lactation as well. So we know that the virus locates in sweat glands, and it actually produces spike protein in the sweat glands. That's been shown in people who've got the serious COVID infection, not the vaccine. So presumably, they're located there because of the ACE-2 receptor being prevalent in those glands. We don't know. Presumption needs to be tested. But we do know that it heavily accumulates there and that's probably the only mechanism by which it could take place. So, if in fact, that is, heavy expression of the ACE-2 receptor for the spike protein now, after vaccination, not the virus, but the excess spike protein.

If that is concentrated in sweat glands, obviously, there's a possibility of that getting into the surface of the skin, and evaporating and creating an aerosol. Now, that very possibility was actually discussed in a paper that came out of Wuhan and as a matter of fact, by some pathologists who would autopsy a person who died of COVID. And they were drawing attention to the fact that transmission by perspiration as they call it, let's now call it, to aerosolization, could be a problem for the virus now that we're talking about. Now let's talk now about the vaccine. What is ominous about this is that in the Pfizer submission, for the trial data, for the trial that they did that they began circulating to the CDC, they seem to have envisaged that very problem, which makes that even more sinister. They were actually said in print, look out for this possibility but, they also said do not report it as part of the vaccine, as a vaccine reaction, report it separately to the trial coordinator. As if they were anticipating the possibility of this happening. So, if you put all these strands together, Pfizer seems to have thought that it's possible.

We have evidence of Chinese pathologists saying the virus itself can be, can get into sweat and quite possibly into saliva, too, by the way. The missing parts in the theory are with each progressive step along that way, getting into someone that then breathes it in and has an effect on them as a bystander. What's the dose? It will be progressively reduced in each step. That's the first problem. The second problem is, although we know about how the virus gets into the body through these ACE-2 receptors in the throat in the upper respiratory tract, there'd been no studies as to how an inhaled spike protein might get in. We don't know that.

Dr. Sam Dubé: Or even physical contact on the surface of the skin, right? Like, we don't know if there's a mechanism there.

Dr. Roger Hodkinson: We just don't know. So I mean, you could consider, you know, you shake hands with someone who's, you know, just been vaccinated and you're playing around with your nose or you're picking your nose or whatever. You know, who knows how this, all I'm saying is...

Dr. Sam Dubé: Kissing someone.

Dr. Roger Hodkinson: It's a hypothesis that has some reason to be considered and the fact that it was in the Pfizer submission makes it all the more ominous.

Dr. Sam Dubé: Yeah, I mean.

Dr. Roger Hodkinson: Yeah, these 1000s of women may not be wrong, and what's also interesting is, of course, many of these women that are coming down without normal periods are post-menopausal, you know, it happens as we know, right?

Dr. Sam Dubé: Sometimes very rarely.

Dr. Roger Hodkinson: It happens.

Dr. Sam Dubé: I saw it at the women's centre, you know, once in a while.

Dr. Roger Hodkinson: Without saying you got cancer or anything, it happens. But we also know that the expression of the ACE-2 receptor in the endometrium, the lining of the uterus, we also know from before COVID that the expression of that goes up the older a woman is. And therefore, again, you could imagine an increased likelihood in older women coming down with that interference with the blood supply, that very fragile blood supply of the lining of the uterus. So, emphasized, underlined, okay. No scaremonger, not proven by any means but worthy of study, like so many other things in this mess. It's not being done.

Dr. Sam Dubé: No, you're not coming across as a fear monger at all. Roger, you're coming across as being objective, experienced, and having a lot of common sense as well. You know, and what can we do as a people now to protect, I mean, they're arresting priests.

Dr. Roger Hodkinson: Excuse me. Not just arresting them. A pastor in in Alberta was supposed to kneel on the road, in the rain, with cars zooming by, and it was put through the indignity of having handcuffs put on him, kneeling on the road, and then dragged off by his boots, and put in the back of a police cruiser to be placed on a slab in a jail for three days with the light on all the time. Maxime Bernier was arrested in Manitoba for having the audacity to address a protest meeting.

Dr. Sam Dubé: Yes.

Dr. Roger Hodkinson: The man who could have been Prime Minister had things to about…

Dr. Sam Dubé: Yes, he was very close.

Dr. Roger Hodkinson: And that that order would have come directly from Pallister. You cannot do that without the guy at the top knowing exactly what's going on.

Dr. Sam Dubé: A man who avoided that ivermectin question, by taking a big gulp of water, looking very uncomfortable shuffling some papers, and then commenting about we're gonna manufacture vaccines in Canada someday soon. How more blatant can you get?

Dr. Roger Hodkinson: Let me paint the really big picture of what's going on here for everyone. So, the politicians create this pseudo pandemic, this pandemic of fear, they created, they actually created that. And then they said, you know, this is so bad, we're going to have to introduce all these auditory measures, which you know, don't work, but it's gonna protect my backside because it shows that I'm doing something. And they double down on it when it didn't work, and double down and extended it. And so on. I mean, you know, Einstein's statements of stupidity, something we repeat over and over again, expect the outcome to be different.

Dr. Sam Dubé: Different, yes.

Dr. Roger Hodkinson: Okay. So they put us through this nightmare of suppression, and indignity, wearing diapers on our faces for the whole year. And then they have the gall to say we're only gonna take the dogs off if you stupid lot get vaccinated with an experimental vaccine to put your lives on the line to get us off the hook of doing things that we knew didn't work. That's the big picture that's going on here, and then they say, just to be sure, yeah, of course you don't have to take that vaccine. Oh, no, we'd never do that, that's against human rights, isn't it? But you won't be able to travel if you don't you make your minds up, you stupid lot. That's what they say, and then at the end of that story, having created this huge mess, and massive economic disruption, needing to be supported with money coming out of taxpayers' pockets. They bring up the most massive incremental debt this country's ever seen out of war time that our children will have to pay for a mess that they created. That's been a knock on consequences of this whole thing.

Dr. Sam Dubé: Yes. You've mentioned to me you're concerned about the, I mean, not to mention all the other consequences the economic consequences, the social consequences. Can we talk about it for a moment?

Dr. Roger Hodkinson: In Britain, the incremental national debt over what it was directed due to COVID. The incremental national debt in Britain is three times the annual budget of the entire National Health Service for one condition; the general public hadn't a clue about what zeros mean. Billions mean. You know, politicians are just getting away with murder here for our future generations to pay for, not just with. I mean, it's not the cash; the cash will come out of increased taxes, subtexts, reduced standard of living, and/or reduced services subjects, lower quality health care, subtexts, poor education, subtexts, poorer police. Those are the consequences of massive borrowing because you cannot default on the debt and or you, you undergo devaluation. And so our children, even if they survive this attempt to sterilize them, potentially. Our children are not just part of this whole cascade of madness themselves, but they are going to be paying for it.

Dr. Sam Dubé: Yes.

Dr. Roger Hodkinson: But that's okay.

Dr. Sam Dubé: To them yeah.

Dr. Roger Hodkinson: I don't think so. It's the maddest episode in human history. It's at a scale that nothing else could match in terms of the number of people that are being, as we speak, being injected with an experimental substance. And at Nuremberg, seven so-called physicians swung for doing much less than that.

Dr. Sam Dubé: Yes. Are we going to be able to hold the people making policy accountable? And if so, how, Roger?

Dr. Roger Hodkinson: They think they can hide behind statutory immunity that you can't sue a bureaucrat or you can't sue a politician. Well, I think they've got a big surprise coming to them because that's going to be tested in court, whether that's blanket 100%, or whether it could have certain understandable limitations, given the scale of what's underway. And not being able to deny knowledge–deniable plausibility.

Dr. Sam Dubé: Oh, yes. Right. Plausible deniability. Yeah.

Dr. Roger Hodkinson: I think they are up for a big surprise, not just in politics, but boards, government, schools, for example. And companies, boards of directors of companies, for example, that are saying be vaccinated or don't show up. Because I understand from other people that it's getting incredibly expensive now to buy directors' liability insurance.

Dr. Sam Dubé: Yes.

Dr. Roger Hodkinson: And a lot of companies are going naked into the night on that. And they could be very surprised with the consequences of their actions and that's where notices of liability come to the fore, I think...

Dr. Sam Dubé: Something people can do to protect themselves. We talked about this before.

Dr. Roger Hodkinson: It's cheap, it's immediate, but more importantly, it's very threatening. What you're doing is they're threatening you, and so you're saying to them, listen, I'm putting you on notice here. If something terrible happens to me or my child, such as this, this, and this, I'm putting you on notice that you cannot deny that you were ignorant of what you were doing. And if these terrible things happen, I'm putting you on notice with this letter that you personally will be sued. Have I got your attention yet? Now, it's likely not many people will not follow through with that, obviously, class action suit. So this is going to be a bonanza for lawyers, obviously, over the next decade, unbelievable bonanza for lawyers. But for the individual receiving that notice of liability, it could be a great shot across the bow. Holy shit, am I personally liable for this? Let me think that through for a minute.

Dr. Sam Dubé: You know, Roger, we had this vaccine act in 1986, which basically took away liability for the most part for vaccine companies. Is it possible like you know, I'm not the most politically oriented guy, I'm not the most legally oriented guy. Is it possible that the powers that be i.e. the current Biden administration, might be able to pass some sweeping grand legislation that oh, no employer can be held liable for any vaccine damages, because, you know, we had to mandate them for this national emergency, and therefore, you have no recourse whatsoever. Is that a possibility?

Dr. Roger Hodkinson: I don't think they're gonna roll that blanket immunity back. I can't see that happening at all.

Dr. Sam Dubé: What I mean is, like, you could have this notice of liability to scare an employer into many parts that look, you're just like the Methodist in the hospital in Texas, right. So, they mandated that their employees have to get the vaccine and there were like 117-plus of them that got on this lawsuit, basically saying, you're not going to do that. If you're telling us to sign and it's perfectly safe, then why don't you also say that you'll cover any damages? Because they wouldn't, they wouldn't do that. So they were contradicting themselves. Right. So, what I'm saying is, if an employer can mandate, could there be some overarching law passed that says no, employers are no longer, they would not be held liable at all? In other words, making moot what you just said about lawyers having a field day? I'm just wondering, I don't know. I wouldn't

Dr. Roger Hodkinson: That could, be I mean, that the immunity was, was only extended to the manufacturers of the vaccine.

Dr. Sam Dubé: And you're saying they would never roll that. Okay. Well…

Dr. Roger Hodkinson: I doubt that they'd roll that back, but there would be enormous comfort for the population to be told that employers, if they want to do that, cannot hide behind any immunity, that they're very much responsible for the consequences. And that, of course, extends to vaccine passports as well, that, you know, the government should not do the, that kind of weaselly thing of saying, oh, we don't want to touch that. You know, we don't want to mandate vaccine passports, but if any company wants to do that, to walk into Walmart one day, we're just going to say it's your decision. You know, that would be an abrogation of government's responsibility. They should prohibit companies from employers from mandating vaccination as a massive intrusion of our privacy. And, you know, we don't have people walking around with "I'm HIV positive" plastered or tattooed on their forehead, you know.

Dr. Sam Dubé: No.

Dr. Roger Hodkinson: It's a very private thing. What your personal health status is, what your vaccination status is. Eventually that will get tested in the courts, of course, and it'll get tossed out as a gross intrusion of human rights, but...

Dr. Sam Dubé: Yeah, and people are going around now you go outside and you see people you haven't seen in a while, why do you get your vaccine? Yeah. And it's like, have you got your STD test yet? You know, like I might as well just ask.

Dr. Roger Hodkinson: I think the best rebuttals to that is a famous cartoon where you see two rats in a cage and, you know, one rat saying to the other rat, have you had your vaccine yet? And the other rat says, of course not, it's not been tested on humans yet.

Dr. Sam Dubé: Or I just tell people, I'm in the control group, or that I self-identify as 100% vaccinated, but that opens up a whole new can of worms. I won't talk about that right. Two other things I didn't want to, want to talk to you about while I have you here, Roger, captive is the concept of natural immunity, herd immunity, and also the variants. So, you look at the CDC site, and they've retconned, as we say, their statements about herd immunity and natural meeting now, apparently, natural immunity isn't the thing.

And herd immunity can only occur through vaccination, whereas in medical school, we were taught something pretty different.

Dr. Roger Hodkinson: These "vaccines" are giving immunity to direct immunity against simply the spike protein. That's it, the spikes that stick out on this virus, well, the spikes that stick out in this virus, it's the whole virus at all, there's all kinds of other...

Dr. Sam Dubé: ...Right...

Dr. Roger Hodkinson: All kinds of other proteins on that, on that vaccine on that virus that the immune system if you had a real COVID infection, which of course we know, is very rare. But the real COVID infection, you're developing immunity to every single element of the virus, not just the spike protein. And so, natural immunity is much more effective than limited immunity to simply the spike protein and herd immunity with things that are not the Ebola category. But herd immunity is normally created the natural way with upper respiratory tract infections anyway, like the flu, in that we give it to each other accidentally in the course normal living, and we develop enough people that got the infection that it helps to control it in the future. It's cheap, it's safe, it's immediately available, it's the way it's normally done, other than with directed vaccinations against measles and mumps and hepatitis and that kind of thing. No, we have no solution to upper respiratory tract virus pandemics; we have no solution at all. Modern medicine is totally impotent at controlling this. And politicians just can't get their mind around that, you know. They want to be the natural saviour of the world without recognizing that we can do nothing.

Dr. Sam Dubé: And then take credit when there's some positive effects, of course. Right, exactly. And these variants, you know, if I remember SARS, 2003. Okay, where is SARS today?

Dr. Roger Hodkinson: It resides in some vials in level four labs in Wuhan, and in the States and in Canada, of course. Bio level four lab, right slap bang in the middle of Winnipeg. That was a brilliant place to put it wasn't it.

Dr. Sam Dubé: The middle of the country, yeah, almost.

Dr. Roger Hodkinson: Yeah, so yeah. So it still exists, it did escape a couple of times, it was well contained, it's not emerged since then as a significant problem.

Dr. Sam Dubé: What about MERS?

Dr. Roger Hodkinson: Yeah, MERS is a really bad one that didn't turn out to be a pandemic. We're very fortunate there because the mortality was about 30%. No, it's the variants just a little whoops, sorry. RNA viruses mutate all the time. We know that it's dogma, you can't stop it. It's the fact that they're not very good at copying each other themselves. And so errors get introduced without correction, like they do when we're copying DNA, and so these RNA viruses will always be ahead of the game. You can't stop them mutating.

Dr. Sam Dubé: Right.

Dr. Roger Hodkinson: And these, again, you see, it's scare-mongering, you know, it's the "double mutants".

Dr. Sam Dubé: Right?

Dr. Roger Hodkinson: It's, they appear, you know, from, you know, sewers in the ground and consume you, you know, you know that... that's scaremongering because these variants, even if they're more transmissible, I say to that, so what? It's meaningless; in fact, it's a good idea, because we want to build herd immunity to the natural way. It's not something to be scared of. First of all, it can't be stopped. Second, it's something we have to accommodate to. And thirdly, it's building herd immunity anyway because the immune system is going to recognize all these variants essentially coming from the same family, and it will attack them all at the same time.

Dr. Sam Dubé: Yeah. And that's what natural immunity.

Dr. Roger Hodkinson: The percentage variation of the genome of these variants as...

Dr. Sam Dubé: Yeah, I think he said, 0.3% is the biggest.

Dr. Roger Hodkinson: Not 0.3, but three 3%.

Dr. Sam Dubé: Oh, point 3%, excuse me.

Dr. Roger Hodkinson: But still very low.

Dr. Sam Dubé: Your immune system can compensate for that.

Dr. Roger Hodkinson: Insignificant difference. Our immune system is miraculously efficient, recognizing common aspects of an invader, and will kill them all.

Dr. Sam Dubé: And Dr. Mike Yeadon, didn't you mention that also, that SARS-**CoV**-2 shares about 80% genetic similarity to SARS?

Dr. Roger Hodkinson: Yes.

Dr. Sam Dubé: And about 60% to the common cold.

Dr. Roger Hodkinson: Yeah.

Dr. Sam Dubé: And there's definitely some overlap in the way your immune system works.

Dr. Roger Hodkinson: Yes. And not only that, but we know that people that did get SARS, their antibodies are still around, you know, however, many years it was ago.

Dr. Sam Dubé: And Spanish Flu too right, like there was some kind of reaction still yeah and wow.

Dr. Roger Hodkinson: And remember, that's just the antibodies, which are the minor aspect of how we counter viral infections. The main defense is cellular immunity with lymphocytes, T lymphocytes that have a memory of what they've met before and don't like something that's not you getting into your body, and a virus, and they knock it off with incredible efficiency.

Dr. Sam Dubé: Right. The reason why Roger, I mentioned SARS and MERS is because I just wanted to ask you what's the natural progression of mutation of these coronaviruses, I mean, aren't the majority mutations like weakening to the, and then to get a truly more virulent strain, is much more rare because you can kill the host right? And you don't **[Inaudible 35:10]**.

Dr. Roger Hodkinson: Historically, mutations in RNA viruses tend to weaken it progressively because, as you said, from an evolutionary perspective, it's not a good idea to kill the person that you're trying to grow in, you know, I don't think viruses think that way. But that's the way it seems to have played out, historically. So, the bottom line is that these variants are nothing to worry about to keep you awake at night, you know, the mutants going to come out of the plugs in the wall and attack you. No, please stop the fearmongering, stop exaggerating everything you possibly can in order to intimidate people knowing full well that you've got them under their, under your thumb. It's despicable how they're constantly emphasizing the negative instead of the assuaging fear, and giving people the real story about how they should be able to go along with their normal lives. And hug people and shake hands and smile and go on holiday and do all the, you remember the time when we did all of that?

Dr. Sam Dubé: It seems like a distant memory now Roger.

Dr. Roger Hodkinson: It was called a time called BC. Before COVID a time called BC, before COVID. We will remember this time as the time of the most supreme idiocy the world has ever seen.

Dr. Sam Dubé: I really hope so, Roger.

Dr. Roger Hodkinson: It's even worse than the tulip bulb mania in the 1600s.

Dr. Sam Dubé: Dr. Geert Vandenbosch, in publishing that open letter, and his background in vaccines and virology, he was very concerned about the vaccines. One of them stopped because of the potential to create I think variants now. Is there any? Can we talk about that? Is there... What do we know?

Dr. Roger Hodkinson: I think that's farfetched. I mean, it could be given the randomness of it. It certainly could be that quite naturally, one of these RNA viruses could mutate into something, it's Armageddon. I mean, there's no way. I mean, that's, that's a statistical game of chance. The vast majority of mutations in a virus that's been around for probably millennia, the vast majority of mutations, are not necessarily conducive to living longer, being more infectious. The vast majority of mutations that take place randomly, that's something that's more likely than not to be negative, rather than having a terrible consequence.

Dr. Sam Dubé: So, this is what I thought happened.

Dr. Roger Hodkinson: Sorry.

Dr. Sam Dubé: This is what I thought happened to SARS. I thought that there was a kind of herd immunity and a dying off weakening of the virus and I don't know, but...

Dr. Roger Hodkinson: No, I think I think we got rid of SARS, largely because of the interval between the exposure and infection was very short. And we were able to contain it much more effectively.

Dr. Sam Dubé: Now, what about the possibility of, you know, destroying your immune system with the vaccines that Dr. Vandenbosch was alluding to, or expressly stating, there was a potential danger with trying to you know, replace natural broad spectrum immunity that would give you natural immunity to you know, 1400 plus epitopes of COVID-19 versus very specific immunity to certain, you know, strains and then.. your immune system. You don't buy that?

Dr. Roger Hodkinson: I don't buy that. The immune system is the 11th wonder of the world. It's complexity, its efficiency are unbelievable, its majesty. When you think of the reality, Sam, that every day, every second of our lives, until we die in our eighties, we've got shit going through our intestine that's separated from the blood vessels by one cell thick. With probably millions of penetrations every day, with bugs that could kill us and we don't die. Do we?

Dr. Sam Dubé: No.

Dr. Roger Hodkinson: Despite having a belly full of shit for 80 years, we don't die.

Dr. Sam Dubé: Spoken like a pathologist.

Dr. Roger Hodkinson: That speaks to the incredible efficiency of our immune system.

Dr. Sam Dubé: Yeah.

Dr. Roger Hodkinson: 100%, not 99.999% 100% efficient, for 80 years, despite all the many and various pathogens that could come in, probably 1000s of them. We knock them off like that.

Dr. Sam Dubé: So Roger, as a medical educator, in addition to your other credentials, what are they teaching the kids in medical school today, because it seems to fly in the face of, you know, what, the response flies in the face of, you know, the standard medical curricula, natural immunity, herd immunity, this incredibly sophisticated and effective immune system that you just described, protecting us from shit, you know, that we're in very close contact on a daily basis, over 80 years.

Dr. Roger Hodkinson: I saw it close up and personal spending 15 years teaching medical students and residents. There's been a morphing of the type of person that goes into medicine, you know, they're now more infatuated with the title and the money than they are with the principle ethics of helping society, avoiding harm. There's been a tendency to practice medicine by numbers, by investigations instead of that precious, valuable time of actually talking to the patient, listening to them, listening to the credibility, the patent and all the information that we can get out of an extended history. Very little from examination, as you know. Tests are basically used to confirm the hypothesis that you've already formed from listening to them. So, there's a tendency by the younger generations of physicians to practice medicine by numbers and I used to teach them just by cranking out numbers in the lab all the time. I used to teach them, you know, don't practice by numbers, please. You know, look at the whole patient, the whole patient, and hold the evidence out here at arm's length, half close your eyes, put it into your, in your computer, press a button, that's called the probability analysis of every single bit of information that you've heard and seen and read.

And lo and behold, you get a list in order of priorities of what you think the likely diagnosis is. I used to teach the medical medicine is not a science. Medicine is the art of applied statistics and you don't know you're doing it. If you're a seasoned physician, you don't know you're applying that principle with every single input, every single word, a smile on the face, how they walk in, sit down, what you've got in the file, you know. So many inputs to form an informed, to have an informed opinion on what's likely, because you and I know in medicine, if you start investigating the 100th cause of everything, the system will go bankrupt. So, I had the deep... having been a general practice before I went into pathology, I had the deepest appreciation of the difficulty of being an excellent GP because you're riding by the seat of your pants, and you will be wrong. Because you've been a responsible doctor, didn't want to break the bank, because you can't rule out everything.

Dr. Sam Dubé: No, you certainly can't and...

Dr. Roger Hodkinson: General practice is the hardest job in medicine.

Dr. Sam Dubé: I've met some real angels in general practice.

Dr. Roger Hodkinson: Because what you're really doing is 90% of the time you're not making diagnoses at all, you're ruling out disease, and what medical students don't realize is when you've got someone sitting in front of you, there's an unspoken word, always for a new condition. There's always an unspoken word, cancer.

Dr. Sam Dubé: Yes.

Dr. Roger Hodkinson: Right, cancer. You know, I am scared, the real purpose of general practice is not to make diagnoses, it's to make scared people feel better.

Dr. Sam Dubé: It's so funny my preceptor and family medicine. My main preceptor once said to me, family medicine is about in my belief about 85% reassurance.

Dr. Roger Hodkinson: Absolutely.

Dr. Sam Dubé: You know [**cross-talking**].

Dr. Roger Hodkinson: People will never express their fear.

Dr. Sam Dubé: That is so true. And there's some really good people in medicine and as you mentioned, there's a different complexion now. If you could give advice to medical students today, during these times, medical students, perhaps that want to make a real difference, what would you tell them, Roger?

Dr. Roger Hodkinson: Remember the guiding principles of medicine: you're here to serve humanity, not yourself. It's difficult sometimes.

Dr. Sam Dubé: Yeah. And that's great advice for any physician. What? Sorry.

Dr. Roger Hodkinson: No, it's something that makes me quite emotional, actually.

Dr. Sam Dubé: What else would you say to practicing physicians or research physicians regarding what's going on today?

Dr. Roger Hodkinson: If you don't stand up, and you're knowledgeable, you're part of the problem; you should be ashamed of yourselves. You should not be considering the personal consequences; you should be considering humanity, should be considering children, you should be looking at the big picture. That's why you have the title, that's why you have the respect, that's why you have the income. You have to; you have to accept the responsibility, the deep responsibility that comes along with the title. You're not, you're not there just to make fancy rare diagnoses and you know and a lot of money. No, that's not why you're there, that will, that will happen if you live by those ethics and you're hardworking, and you develop rapport with your patients, and they actually want to come back to you because you're living those ethics. That's what I'd recommend — soul searching before you start, because if you're not prepared to follow that path, you're not really a physician.

Dr. Sam Dubé: No, when you get bureaucrats like Fauci who are in a position of, let's face it, power and influence, where people hang on his words, his advice. And now we see these emails, but you know, we knew for a long time that he was incredibly inconsistent and arbitrary. And now the emails are starting to show that more. What I'm interested in is redacted material in the emails.

Dr. Roger Hodkinson: Very much so.

Dr. Sam Dubé: But then you can't help but think about the ego in the, let's be honest here, there. You know, there's some narcissistic traits, especially when one declares that if you're going against Anthony Fauci, you're going against science. What science is a person? What?

Dr. Roger Hodkinson: Yeah, no, he's lost his way, he's out of his depth; he's not really had much real world medical experience with patients. He's looking upon this as simultaneously, you know, a, an academic issue. He's undoubtedly very smart, he's quite accomplished, but he doesn't really get the essence of medicine, which is the humanity that I was talking about. He's lost his way and, you know, he's digging himself in all the time, how to extricate because of the actions that he's taken are just untenable. It's very tragic to see his career end, and in this way, because he will be unquestionably. He is going to have a fall.

Dr. Sam Dubé: Really. So, a bureaucrat like Fauci, you can understand the power, the money he has vested financial interest, very clearly huge conflict of interest here going on. But what about the clinicians out there right now that are in positions to, you know, report adverse effects on VAERS? They're in positions to give advice. What is the psychological process going on here with those who are drinking the Kool Aid so to speak? Can you speak to that a little bit? Just give us some insight into what you think is going on here. I mean, we're all human, right, Roger? But still...

Dr. Roger Hodkinson: It's very simple at the end of the day, given the power of the colleges. It's income versus ethics, and income is winning. Sadly, it's been a change in the makeup of the profession. And I think the willingness to submit, and follow the crowd is perhaps a general symptom of what you might call "woekism," you know, not daring to be different and yet, assuming that the norm, so to speak, the commonality is so prevalent, that I'm going to follow it without even any serious thought. You know, just because you're a physician doesn't mean to say you're well read or up to date, and it doesn't mean that you're necessarily going to be following evidence-based medicine. And you may be so concerned with your the realities of maintaining your family's income that you put all those things aside, even though you may have a gut feeling that there's something very wrong here. It's a sad commentary, isn't it?

Dr. Sam Dubé: It is.

Dr. Roger Hodkinson: On physicians that they're not willing to do that. That's why I so admire the likes of Dr. Patrick, who is, you know, the tall poppy they just, they're gonna knock off his head because the system. Dr. Bhakdi, the most prominent academic, you might say, immunologist in the world in Germany, has been getting death threats. He's thinking of leaving Germany. It's that serious?

Dr. Sam Dubé: He sounded the alarm very early on, didn't he?

Dr. Roger Hodkinson: And, you know there are consequences, not just losing income, but there are consequences of your own personal safety when you speak up. So, I admire him deeply for taking that stand. That was incredibly brave, and he's young guy, he's got his career ahead of him, you know?

Dr. Sam Dubé: Yeah. Dr. Patrick Phillips? Yes.

Dr. Roger Hodkinson: That takes real balls.

Dr. Sam Dubé: Absolutely. Oh, my God. Yeah. It really does. And...

Dr. Roger Hodkinson: He wasn't just speaking up, he was in Parliament.

Dr. Sam Dubé: Yes. He was in Parliament, along with Dr. Welsh and Dr. Bridle and Derek Sloan. And this is very recent; this was a couple of days ago. Umm...

Dr. Roger Hodkinson: By the way, he sits separately at a different, on a different occasion with respect to the Canadian adverse reaction system of reporting. He had submitted, I think he said six adverse reaction reports, five of them were rejected, coming from a physician. And the reason they were rejected, get this from, you know, the ultimate, you know, bureaucratic idiocy, the, I call it, well in a moment, I call it I've got some unkind words for that. Yes, he got rejected because the form that he was supposed to fill in did not have the lot number of the vaccine on it. Is any bureaucrat listening? Adverse reactions happen after you leave the place where you've been injected. Other than the severe anaphylactic reactions, which happen under your face the remote in time. Hello. You expect the system to be functional? If you want that data before you've accepted it — are you off another planet?

Dr. Sam Dubé: Unbelievable. It's like purposely making it difficult or impossible to report.

Dr. Roger Hodkinson: Yeah, we don't know. And therefore, if we don't know we can't be... we can't be said to be responsible for the consequences. That's why, when in Alberta, with a court case going on here, when the, I don't think it was the medical officer of health itself, it might well have been actually, or one of the minions, doesn't really matter. They were asked, well, where's the evidence for all of this? To which they said, actually, we don't haven't quite had enough time to put it together. You're telling me that you've been doing this stuff for a year and you haven't been monitoring it? The answer is, you haven't been monitoring it, have you?

Dr. Sam Dubé: Right.

Dr. Roger Hodkinson: Because you didn't want to know, did you? That's why you don't have the data, isn't it? That's how I would have aggressively done the cross-examination.

Dr. Sam Dubé: Yeah, I would have liked for you to have been in Parliament maybe next time, Derek Sloan says anything...

Dr. Roger Hodkinson: They just don't want to know, you see, that's gonna be part of their defence. Oh, you're kidding me all this stuff was going on....

Dr. Sam Dubé: That's the other thing I want to talk to you about is the passing of the buck. I mean, how much of the passing of the buck can happen here, Roger? And this is why I get concerned about accountability and people getting wrapped up in the, you know, the so called legislation and I, we didn't know and it's like, we're not following it, or we don't have any data on that. Or, you know, it's like when the head of the CDC was asked by Senator Dr. Paul Rand, ah, excuse me. No, it was Senator John Kennedy. Can you get me this information? Well, you should talk to Dr. Fauci. No, Dr. Fauci seems to be confused. You're head of the CDC, can you get me this information? Right? Like passing of the buck, like what the heck?

Dr. Roger Hodkinson: But the truth will out, it's inescapable. The madness is on such a scale, that it will be documented chapter and verse in books that will be coming out very shortly before the court cases resolve any of these matters. Reputations are going to be slaughtered because of the ample evidence that's now available to be rolled out the full litany of the problems from start to finish. It's unavoidable, it's tragic that we had to go through this year of madness in order to document all of that, but it will be documented, and the truth always comes out, no matter how much you want to hide it. The truth will come out, and people like Fauci, sadly, are going to have their reputations absolutely trashed.

Dr. Sam Dubé: Well, there were definitely some choices made there on his end. So you know, you said, come fall, we don't know what's going to happen, right?

Dr. Roger Hodkinson: It's anyone's guess, right? How it, if it comes back, does it come back? What happens to the flu but the big danger there, of course, is that revisiting this whole madness all over again, you know masks and booster shots and against variants and, you know, vaccine passports might actually have started to take hold. We don't know.

Dr. Sam Dubé: This is what I'm concerned with Roger.

Dr. Roger Hodkinson: So we are looking at creating an organiz-ation that takes that long-term view and not just children, which are the urgent matter right now. But in the fall, this isn't going, the politics of this are not going to disappear in the fall. The danger is that they could come back in some similar guise. And there's a desperate need for a global organization here that pulls together all the strands so that ordinary people get informed about what's going on with appropriate messaging, backed by individuals, substantial credentials, doctors. I'm talking about a doctors organization now. And you know, there are moves afoot to start something along those lines, which I'm privy to, and I hope it takes off because you can't fight a juggernaut with a pea shooter. You have to have a scalable organization that is commensurate with the scale of the problem. Other than that, if you don't have that, you're simply you know, you're not going to move the needle.

Dr. Sam Dubé: So Roger, I believe that throughout all this, a big chunk of the public has lost faith in their physicians, public health authorities in general, even the, you know, the government. Can things ever go back or improve? And what do we have to go through in order for that to occur? I'm skeptical.

Dr. Roger Hodkinson: Yes, so am I. Reputations are earned over years or decades, and they can be lost in a second. It takes a while to grovel back and get back what you once had. If you're even partially culpable here, you know, people will remember the next election I think, who's responsible for this. As I said, heads will roll in various ways, whether it's because of elections or whether it's because of organizational structure, bureaucrats being fired, many medical officers of health being fired. They should all be fired in my opinion because they practice the most terrible medical malpractice hiding behind the skirts of assumed immunity. All these medical officers of health should lose their jobs. Of course they won't. They'll be simply reassigned. Bureaucrats never get fired, do they?

Dr. Sam Dubé: No.

Dr. Roger Hodkinson: So, yeah, it's, I agree. And there could be some adverse vaccination consequences too because, you know, what we don't want is for the general public to think that all vaccines are bad. Many vaccines are good, they're outstanding at preventing disease. And that would be a terrible consequences if there was reluctance to get children vaccinated against some of the obvious things. I hope that doesn't happen, but you're right it's going to be a great reset if you might say, other than the economic reset, that could be a reset of the perception that people have of the profession, the perception they have of the media, perhaps more so than the profession, because the media is going to be seen to be one of the principal enforces here, one of the principle liars of maintaining the narrative. And of course, the sooner some of those media outlets go down, like, you know, completely biased coverage up here, and blatantly biased coverage in Britain. And you know, the similar organizations in the States. Yeah, if they go down because of this, excellent, because they'd be maintaining, not just this narrative, but the woke narrative as well, which is perhaps even more sinister than anything that we've gone through.

Dr. Sam Dubé: Yes, I agree. I agree. You know, there was a reporter a few days ago, Ivory Hecker, who was an investigative reporter for eight years and working for Fox affiliate in Houston, Texas, who came on air and said, hey, you know I'm going to blow the whistle, basically. I've got recordings of my bosses suppressing information and stories that are valuable to the public specifically. You know, she talked later about hydroxychloroquine and how she was told she was a bad reporter. She had a defamation; she had a letter basically that had been put as a warning in her file and she threatened a defamation lawsuit and they had to get rid of it. And she realized that there were things happening, and that this is all out there now. And if all things go well, I'll be interviewing her very shortly, but we need more of that happening too, among the lay people, among the people who are not clinically or research trained to, you know, kind of just sit and gather information, look around and look around and be willing to accept that, wow, there are a lot of bad things happening here because they don't judge.... instead of turning a blind eye, you know? And it's very sad and it's hurtful when, you know, you have really good friends that, you know, you think you know them and they think they know you. And then they say, well, you know, I wanted to travel. So I took the poke, you know?

Dr. Roger Hodkinson: Yeah. And in medicine, you know, the strange thing that›s been going on is that, in normal times, whether you›re talking about statins or whatever, in normal times, there's an open debate in which the pros and cons that's the essence of medicine, how medicine progresses, is argument, it's debate, until eventually there's a consensus in the meta-analysis, and it's shown to be the good thing to do. And everyone buys into it. How can you achieve that kind of consensus if the debate is being intentionally prohibited by the very body that's supposed to be regulating medicine?

Dr. Sam Dubé: It's just unfathomable, you know. It's just unfathomable, and it's so blatant, and it's so frustrating, and it's so anger producing, and you can't help but have this feeling of impotence as well. I think I would call it that, impotence. And you know, sometimes I'm up at night just thinking about what the hell, what the hell, things happened we never thought would happen.

Dr. Roger Hodkinson: To be simultaneously, so angry and also depressed at the same time because of the, you know, you and I are talking very openly now and you will have a certain reach with your podcast. And I salute you for that. And I'm so grateful of having the opportunity of talking with you.

Dr. Sam Dubé: I'm so grateful you came to talk with us honestly.

Dr. Roger Hodkinson: But the big picture is as good as you are and as good as I am, it›s a very small fraction of the population that›s going to be hearing this because the usual way of getting information from the mainstream media, from the newspapers, from the politicians and the reporting of the politicians, and from what you might hear from your doctor, you know, you might go along to see your doctor and say, what do you think about statins? You know, and then he'll give you his opinion. But none of that is happening now. It's a massive change in how we, the public, is being informed and controlled. And as I said before, the great resetters are just loving it. And, beyond the great resetters of course, China is loving it. They're seeing disarray. They're seeing the decay of capitalistic principles and democracy and the constraints of freedom. And they're saying to themselves, Hey, we don't have to do a damn thing. They're going to kill themselves, you know?

Dr. Sam Dubé: Yeah. They're doing the job. They're doing the job for us.

Dr. Roger Hodkinson: We're seeing, this is mainly a microcosm of the decay of democracy and capitalism. It's just a little piece of that unraveling that's been going on for some time. And it doesn't bode well for everything that we hold dear, our freedoms in particular. It does not bode well. It's going to be very interesting. Isn't it? To see what Biden does when the Chinese finally get around to invading Hong Kong.

Dr. Sam Dubé: Oh my God.

Dr. Roger Hodkinson: Yeah. Yeah. That's the toe in the water for the Chinese, what's he going to do? And the answer is he's not going to do anything. It's a please walk right in. It's going to be like the Russians in the Ukraine. And that will give them appetite for Taiwan. And if Trump doesn't get in next time, all bets are off in my opinion.

Dr. Sam Dubé: Yup. I agree, and those are some ominous words Roger. I want to give the opportunity to give us some last words that are maybe a little more hopeful, you know.

Dr. Roger Hodkinson: I will give some hope because the sun is going to come up and, you know, what used to be called the season of coughs and colds, which is actually the season of vitamin D deficiency, that's going to evaporate. And the politicians will say, of course I didn't just wrestle this to the ground for you. I actually made the sun come up too. I'm so omnipotent. Take your vitamin D, consider your notices of liability. Try and be normal. Protest within the limits of being arrested. Hug, smile, congregate, try to regain the normality that we all all had. But while you're doing all that in terms of, you might say, an optimistic outlook, believe nothing you're told. It's all a pack of lies from beginning to end. And you, the general public, with your head screwed on, you're miles ahead of the Faucis of the world. You know what's going on. And I hope this podcast has given you some comfort to support your gut feeling that there's something smelly in the state of Denmark.

Dr. Sam Dubé: With that Roger, I want to thank you for joining us today here on the *Toronto Business Journal*. Dr. Roger Hodkinson ladies and gentlemen. Thank you from the bottom of my heart.

Dr. Roger Hodkinson: It's been my pleasure. Thank you so much, Sam.

Dr. Sam Dubé: The honor and the pleasure was mine. You honour me, sir. You honour me, you honor me. And I look forward to speaking to you again, hopefully with some very positive developments, and thank you, sir. And I will sign off for us and you stay safe and, and please we will stay in touch.

Dr. Roger Hodkinson: Thank you. Bye-Bye.

Appendix 5

Ivory Hecker—A Journalist for the People

Dr. Sam Dubé: Hello, Dr. Sam Dubé here once again for the *Toronto Business Journal*. And I am honored to have with me here today former Fox News reporter, Ivory Hecker. Ivory, thank you so much for joining us today.

Ivory: Thanks for having me.

Dr. Sam Dubé: Now, many of you, especially in the bitchute world, know Ivory quite well, at least over the last few weeks. Ivory whistleblew on her bosses on Fox News for the suppression of information concerning an early treatment modality for COVID-19, and not being the drug of hydroxychloroquine. So, Ivory, it's pretty well-known, your story now. And at least it was all over the internet until YouTube started taking down your videos and including the main one that actually had the detailed recordings of your bosses chastising you, and basically scolding you and telling you, in no uncertain terms, you could no longer pursue this. Can you tell us a little bit, in your own words, what happened?

Ivory: Fox assigned me to cover COVID treatment at a hospital. They disliked what the interview subjects said and proceeded to crucify me for it. They didn't just say, "You can no longer pursue the story we sent you to." They actually said, "You're going to be severely punished, internally ripped apart. And a defamatory letter is placed in your file, so you can no longer move ahead in the company. You're also going to go on a social media blackout. Nothing will be posted without our permission. You don't understand the narrative," so to speak. They didn't say this verbally, but that was their message, "You don't get the narrative, Ivory. Therefore, we're going to teach you the narrative real good with all this crazy disciplinary action." And I said, "Okay, let me get the defamation lawyer." And that's when they backtracked and we're like, "Oh, my gosh, we are so sorry."

But the public needs to know this because this is evidence that narrative news telling is not only real, but it's forced upon innocent journalists. So, when you see news that you don't believe or seems slanted, sometimes it's not even the reporter's fault. Sometimes the reporter is being forced to report a certain way, or at least intimidated into reporting a certain way if they're not attacked as viciously internally as I was.

Dr. Sam Dubé: Now, in that defamation letter, isn't it true that they tried to twist things a little bit?

They tried to change the chronology of events, claiming that they had actually warned you in the past and make it look like there was this kind of paper trail, and then you had to pull out the guns and they were forced to get rid of it? And you provided recordings of HR admitting that they got rid of the letter, and that's it. We're no longer referred to it. They went as far as manipulation, didn't they?

Ivory: Yeah. They created a fake timeline and said that they had banned me from covering COVID drug treatments 2 weeks prior to that story. That wouldn't make much sense for them to ban me from a segment of COVID treatment and then send me to a COVID treatment story without any instruction on what aspect of treatment not to cover. But the fact that they're going to issue that instruction when they did, you should never issue instruction to a journalist to not cover certain facts. Journalists are supposed to collect all the facts and put them out to the public, especially the most important ones. It's just very strange. It's a sad day in journalism.

Dr. Sam Dubé: So, ultimately, you were doing a piece on, I believe this was the air conditioning and the summer heat, something like that, right?

Ivory: Yeah.

Dr. Sam Dubé: And you just let it go. And the clip is infamous. You can still find it on BitChute and Rumble and stuff. And you just very casually expressed that you found a nonprofit user organization, Project Veritas, you'd be releasing the details there, and that you've uncovered significant evidence of cover up and being told not to pursue these things, and basically to manipulate the news, basically to manipulate the facts and not have free speech. So, you were fired. And in fact, you've heard a rumor of your firing. Not uncommon. We've heard about this in the past in Hollywood and other places that were being told, and then finding out, and then getting an official letter, fairly recently, that you posted. Is that correct?

Ivory: Yeah. So, the letter letting me know directly that I've been fired finally showed up yesterday through snail mail. But a week ago, I heard the rumor that I was fired.

Dr. Sam Dubé: How did you feel at that point? And let me contextualize this, because on Project Veritas, you had said something about you'd been trying to figure out a way to get fired or leave your job for 10 months, something like that. Because this had this has been going on for a long time, right? Like this original incident was in the summer of 2020. Is that correct? And that's almost a year ago. And so, were you feeling trapped in any way? Were you feeling...?

Ivory: Absolutely. Yeah.

Dr. Sam Dubé: Can you talk a little bit?

Ivory: Yeah. Here they are telling me that I'm not free to just cover the facts on the ground, that I could be viciously persecuted at any time at their whim. That's the precedent they sent. So, I'm no longer safe in the company, let alone safe to do journalism. And it is very violating feeling. I had been violated and the viewers had been violated. So, I felt a strong need to get out and tell the truth about Fox. And from then on, I've just kind of been trapped within the company in danger, I continue to record. I say in danger because I had been targeted out of left field, apparently because I accidentally happened upon a narrative that the Fox headquarters didn't like. I have 3 different Fox executives telling me that, "This came down from up top." So, I never knowing when that's going to happen again, so I just started recording to protect myself, the lawyer told me to.

And it was definitely a trapped feeling. And wanting to get out. Not knowing how and wanting to tell the public and not knowing how best to do that. And yeah, so I just kind of had no qualms about calling out my bosses on the narrative from there on out. My bosses continued to do some strange things. It's just like the narrative really got rigid when the pandemic started. It was just like this narrative news telling was more glaring than ever. They were just not afraid to stray from the facts more than ever, and just do weird things like issue edicts that, "You shall not put these facts out on social media or online or on TV. Nobody must know these facts." That's pretty creepy as a journalist.

So, I called my bosses out many times, and just basically trying to prevent my own company from committing suicide. Because the viewers see that something strange is going on, they're turning the TV off. The news just feels fake to them. Something's up. So, I was like, "Look, you guys are, first of all, you're ignoring the questions that viewers are screaming in the comment section of social media. And second of all, you're not only not getting answers to those questions, but hiding certain facts. It's very, very strange." There were a lot of stories that were not that way. Most of the crime stories, they put me on a lot of crime. And usually, that was fine. I could cover the story. But not always.

Dr. Sam Dubé: Now, you had received some tips from your viewers. You were talking about people screaming in the comments and personally receiving tips about alternative treatments or early treatments for COVID-19. And was this what prompted you to ask the questions that you did? Was this what motivated you? Or were there more, was there more to that?

Ivory: It's quite interesting. When Fox sent me to cover this hospital, COVID drug treatments were not something I was interested in. Fox had assigned me to my first hydroxychloroquine story two weeks prior to that. Before that, I didn't even pay attention to it. But after I covered that one story, I saw my viewers were very interested in it. They continued to send me messages and comments about hydroxychloroquine. And a lot of them were telling their stories to me. The Houston Fire Department told me that they couldn't get treatment for their firefighters in a traditional... in some of the main establishment hospitals. They were basically giving the firefighters Tylenol and telling them, "Good luck," when they were having severe cases of COVID. So, they were sending them to this doctor who was giving them hydroxychloroquine, and firefighters were getting better. That's just one of quite a few tips I got about hydroxychloroquine. And people just wondering what's really up with it because it had been censored online so harshly.

So, honestly, that day when they sent me to cover Dr. Verona's hospital, I was asking about the capacity issues and everything I could think of. It was quite a dull interview. So, final question. It just popped into my head, "Well, the viewers have been chattering about hydroxychloroquine." So, I just simply asked, "Are you using it?" And was kind of surprising, he said yes. Because the studies had a couple of weeks prior said that it wasn't worth using. So, I thought the viewers would find that interesting. So, I included it in the package. The boss says, "No get that out of the TV package. You need more context." So, I add the context, put it online instead. And that is when the bosses said that I was disobeying them, even though I got the context they told me to get.

See, they come up with these manipulation games kind of saying without saying I'm supposed to pick up their hints that this is something that's not supposed to be covered. And so, my loyalty is not to them, it's to the viewers. If viewers want to know this, I'm going to put it out to the viewers. And it's just that's what they teach you in journalism school. And it is so sad that corporate news that does not abide by journalism. I thought that corporate news and journalism were the same thing. I learned this past year that, at least at Fox, they no longer are.

Dr. Sam Dubé: So, that's actually my next question for you was, you went through formal journalism training, a young Ivory Hecker, and you just express what you were taught there: to be objective, to look at both sides or more than one side, and to look for the scoop, the truth–the truth, find out the truth. And, sadly, you found out that wasn't the case. Now, what were you thinking and feeling leading up to the days prior to you basically making the declaration during the air conditioning story? How was that going for you? And how were you feeling leading up to that?

Ivory: I was continuing to crave some liberty and peace. It's been a soul-crushing experience at Fox. Just being violated like that and knowing that they're doing wrong things to hide certain things from viewers. It's just, it's really a betraying soul crushing feeling. So, I had this craving to get out of Fox and this anxiety about what that separation would look like and what the consequences for that would be. So, I mean, for like a week or 2 leading up to that day, every morning, I would wake up with a sore jaw because I'd been clenching in my sleep. But I just told myself it's the best thing to get out and to spread the word to people."

Dr. Sam Dubé: Ivory... sorry.

Ivory: I had to grin and bear it and do it.

Dr. Sam Dubé: Grin and bear it, right?

Ivory: Yeah.

Dr. Sam Dubé: Sadly, you mentioned the subtext of having to know not to pursue certain things, having to... had you discussed this with colleagues before, other reporters? Was this something that was, "We're not really supposed to talk about this, but..." or, "We should know better,"? Or are some reporters really, they're still looking for the truth like yourself and hoping that you can pursue this without being scolded and chastised? Was there any discussion about this with colleagues?

Ivory: Yeah, I've talked with a couple colleagues before about the slant in the news and how you're kind of expected to not even pitch certain stories. Like, one co-worker had said that he could just tell things about me by what I pitch. And when I pitch stories, I'm pitching the people's story. And there's this broad spread culture. You could ask anyone in any newsroom across America. There is a left, politically left-leaning culture in every newsroom in America. Ask anyone. And so, I don't care about these weird little groupthink slants that newsrooms do. My loyalty is to citizens, every citizen regardless of their political slant. So, if I'm getting serious newsworthy questions from left-leaning viewers, I'm going to pitch that story. Right-leaning viewers, I'm going to pitch that story. I pitch stories that I can tell are newsworthy that my followers want answers to. I'm always pitching a mix of stories that, apparently, to a lot of people, slant to the left and right.

And because I include the right-leaning pitches as well, a bit of a target or like a weird magnifying glass was put on me. According to one of my co-workers, said that they could just kind of tell something about me, that I was pitching to right-leaning viewers' questions along with the left-leaning viewers' questions.

Dr. Sam Dubé: You were being objective, right? You were being objective and trying to provide balance?

Ivory: It's not even about balance, it's about answering all of the community's questions. The right-leaning segment of the audience matters too. Their questions deserve to be answered too. Not just the left-leaning members of the audience. So, I'm constantly looking to answer everybody's questions.

Dr. Sam Dubé: Now, how did Project Veritas get into the picture?

Ivory: So, it's funny, because after I began to be harassed by Fox in August of last year, that's when I got a lawyer involved, started recording. And I mentioned it to a couple of my friends how crazy this is. It's just out of left field. I had a great relationship with my bosses. They value my work. They put me in the A block on the top story almost always. And so, it's not anything personal against me.

Dr. Sam Dubé: Right.

Ivory: Or it was just it didn't make sense. I was mentioning this to my friends, and multiple friends from multiple walks of life mentioned Project Veritas. They were like, "You should let Project Veritas know about this, especially if you've got recordings." And so, I thought about that for a few months, and I was like, "Okay, I guess I'll reach out to them." Well, I sent them a little tip. I guess they never saw it. But as fate would have it, later on and late January, Project Veritas sent me a Twitter DM out of nowhere after I clicked like on one of their tweets. I guess they saw my blue checkmark and said, "Thanks for the follow," and I said, "Thanks for doing journalism." Regardless of what any member of groupthink says about Project Veritas, they are journalists because they actually collect facts through video, audio recordings, and disseminate the public. You can see and hear what's going on through the person's own words and video. And they're also working on getting answers to a lot of the public's questions, the members of the public who are being alienated. Most of the media does alienate a certain segment of the population. And Project Veritas fills that void, to a certain extent. And I know they're not just... they're not actually a politically motivated organization. So, I don't know. I respected some of the work they did. It's intriguing how much they're hated by the establishment media.

Dr. Sam Dubé: Yeah.

Ivory: I don't care. When they reached out to me and said, "Hey, have you witnessed anything?" I said, "Yeah, I sure am witnessing some weird stuff." So, that's, the rest was history. And that's how it went.

Dr. Sam Dubé: So, now you uncovered, I guess, opened a can of worms or uncovered a hornet's nest when you started investigating and realizing it was a suppression of the hydroxychloroquine story and led to something much bigger. Can you talk to us a little bit to that, Ivory?

Ivory: Oh, specifically in the realm of COVID drug treatments?

Dr. Sam Dubé: No, you don't have to go there, because I know you're not endorsing anything. But we do know that you have been pursuing a story independently. And in fact, right prior to this interview, you were doing an upload of a teaser, correct?

Ivory: Yeah, I just put a teaser on my social media about it.

Dr. Sam Dubé: Can you tell us about your story?

Ivory: Sure. So, just a month or so ago, I happened across some data showing that this Dr. Varone–the original guy I got in trouble for covering, which I was just like, "Whatever. That was weird. They sent me to talk to him. I don't know this guy." Well, I happened upon some information about him that shows the death rate at his hospital was dramatically lower than other hospitals. And that really took me back a bit, and I said, "Whoa, if that's true, then whatever, anything he's doing shouldn't be suppressed. We should be shining more light on what he's doing to save lives."

So, I dug more into it, and ended up talking to his patients, to researchers. I got a one-on-one with World Health org as well and just really dug into what he's doing and what doctors are doing on the ground, and then what the establishment says and how the media is reacting. It's an interesting, interesting piece I put together. I'm still finalizing it to put on Telegram later today.

Dr. Sam Dubé: Wonderful, wonderful. I just wanted to get that out of the way because I think that's going to be some great viewing. I looked at your teaser, and I'm really excited about it. This is really refreshing, Ivory, because you're telling me you found out about the suppression. You were chastised, eventually fired after you came out, and you're still pursuing the truth independently. So, that's like, that's a real sign of integrity and a big breath of fresh air. Because you know as well as I do, people have lost faith in the media, like absolutely lost faith in the media. And then to the point of, like you said, screaming on comments and then having to reduce likes and... dislikes, excuse me, not likes but dislikes, and the viewership for some organizations, like CNN has crashed. Even Fox has crashed. And this is a tremendous loss of faith. And even when you look at the medical system and public health authorities, there's a tremendous loss of faith there as well. So, to hear you speak like this is almost a revelation, certainly for some of us who have been kind of monitoring this for like a year, year and a half, and being skeptical. And it's really great to hear this. So, I encourage everyone to watch your story and just support anything that you do. Now, you're not officially working for Project Veritas, are you right now?

Ivory: No, they have not...

Dr. Sam Dubé: They have not made you the offer. Okay.

Ivory: Actually, no. I mean, James mentioned something, but nothing's...

Dr. Sam Dubé: Okay. So, we won't...

Ivory: Honestly, I'm just like... honestly, the situation with Fox feels so much like a bad breakup, and you can't just jump into another relationship.

Dr. Sam Dubé: That's a really good analogy.

Ivory: That is how I feel. I just need a little bit of space, alone time. And obviously, I just have to finish what I feel like was my duty to... if Fox is going to creepily ban me from a story that the viewers want answers to, I just feel like I needed to finish that story. So, I'm putting that out today, and then maybe I'll just take a breather and then be like, "Okay." My passion for journalism is never going to go away. So, I'm going to do something, but I just need a little bit of alone time.

Dr. Sam Dubé: No, and that's good. And you had a fund set up by your mom, actually. And I thought that was really touching. Because you got fired. Like, how do you put bread on the table honestly?

Ivory: Yeah.

Dr. Sam Dubé: So, I encourage people to take a look at that too, and to support you as best as they can.

Ivory: So nice of the public. I thank them so much.

Dr. Sam Dubé: Yeah, but look at what you're doing. You're actually using that time to continue to seek for the truth. So, thank you for doing that. It's not like you're sitting there going just, "Support me. Please help me. I blew the whistle." You're actually... people are like this is an investment in you, and it's paying off. Do you know what I mean? Like, there's a return on investment in Ivory Hecker. That's the way I see it. So, kudos, kudos to you for doing that. Like you're under no obligation to pursue this, but your integrity and the fact that you're a pure journalist at heart, probably going into journalism for the right reasons. And so, that's really commendable. Like I have to say that, that's just wonderful.

Now, I was going to talk a little bit about this aspect of Fox News kind of caving to the woke agenda. Oh, yeah, there, I said it. I'm sorry I said it. And you'd been witness to this for some time. And when we... I tell people, I don't watch the news. But during the 2016 election, it was pretty obvious what was going on with Fox and CNN and this back and forth. And we don't have such a thing in Canada. We don't have such a thing in Canada. We have a minority government and an official opposition. And right now over COVID, with the government response, everyone is in cahoots. Everyone is responding the same way. So, we don't have the red and the blue. We don't have this kind of polarized, call it a dialog if you want. So, we're in a rough, rough shape up here. What I'm hoping is that your actions will inspire others. April, is it April Moss, a CBS reporter, can you tell us a little bit about that?

Ivory: Oh, yeah, her. So, Project Veritas just put her full segment out last night, and I watched it, and it was just, I thought it was a powerful piece about her wanting to stand up for journalism at its essence, what it used to be, minus the narrative. She told me... I didn't know her prior to this, but she was telling me about how her bosses use the same peer pressure tactics that are rampant in newsrooms across America, of pressuring you out of asking the people's questions. That's so wrong. The people had, in the story that she mentioned to me, vaccine questions. I know that most Americans had questions about this new vaccine. And so, she asked some of the hard-hitting questions that a lot of the viewers had had, and afterwards got kind of reprimanded by her boss, which would be the opposite of what happens in a newsroom. Newsrooms should applaud when a journalist asks tough questions that the public wants answers to. It's definitely easier not to ask those questions, but if you're bold enough to stand up for your viewers and get their answers, that should be applauded.

The fact that newsrooms are trying to push journalists away from that is so alarming. And that's why I thought it was important to come forward with my story. And I'm so glad she's coming forward too. My inbox has gotten so many messages from other journalists, most of them people who've already quit because they are so fed up of the same thing happening to them. There's major problems in newsrooms right now that are not being... they're not acting journalistically. And it's a frightening thing when the free press is what fortifies a free society, yet corporate regulators are not allowing their journalists on the ground to fully utilize the First Amendment.

Dr. Sam Dubé: So, there's definitely this financial pressure. Because, I think you talked to this already on another video about the CDC being involved in funding Fox. Is that correct? Please, correct me if I'm wrong on that.

Ivory: Well, yeah, there were some social media and online ads going through Fox's sites. Not just Fox, Houston, but Fox-owned stations across the nation, these pro vaccine ads slapped with the CDC logo. And when I asked the promotions director, Hoff Rendan, he told me those were paid ads. So, he's like, "Oh, those are easy. Those come straight down pre-produced from the CDC. We pop them out, we get paid for them." So, the CDC is funding pro-vaccine agenda according to Ralph. And could that be contributing to the TV stations' pro-vaccine agenda? I don't know. I think a lot of my bosses are just naturally pro vaccine. But they've, have let their own strong desire to get everyone vaccinated interfere with the viewers' questions. And I think what's happened is it has led to less people being vaccinated. Because they are so animated about getting everyone vaccinated, they refuse to acknowledge serious questions. And when the viewers don't get answers to those serious questions, they're more leery of the vaccine. So, more people are not getting vaccinated. It's backfiring what the Fox bosses were wishing. I have such compelling recordings from my bosses of them strategizing on their efforts to shove vaccines down people's throat.

I have hours of recordings. And look, I don't need to be releasing them all. I think my point has been made. But vaccines, they definitely went into the propaganda territory in their coverage of vaccines. They just got way too personally attached to vaccines. It violated a lot of viewer trust.

Dr. Sam Dubé: You know what? Our Canadian Broadcasting Corporation, just about a week and a half, 2 weeks ago, issued a piece of writing, an article, proclaiming that there are no long-term side effects of the vaccine, and that the spike protein is completely safe. And I looked at this, my jaw dropped. I've discussed it with other researchers and physicians, and we're like, "This is a blatant lie. It's a blatant lie by our national broadcaster." And in fact, I'm going to do a video shortly and pull it apart with an attorney from Children's Health Defense, Robert Kennedy's.

Ivory: The long-term studies of Moderna and Pfizer are not complete yet.

Dr. Sam Dubé: Not at all. We're in phase 3 right now. And the initial trials had no pregnant women, no children, and no elderly. They took healthy people because one of the best possible results. And so, typically, you need 5 to 7 years minimum to produce a vaccine like this. No one's ever produced a real successful Coronavirus vaccine. And yet, they're proclaiming this as if it's the truth. And you can't do that. As a scientist, I'll tell you.

Ivory: And then the journalists are too timid to actually challenge the government on that and say, "Wait a minute, do we really know this?" Journalists are way too loyal right now to government officials. They take whatever government officials say as gospel.

Dr. Sam Dubé: I agree. Is it loyalty or fear?

Ivory: It's a combination. Yeah, a lot of journalists live in some fear. But they're also brainwashed to just do what the government says or report what the government says. And it's a probably sprinkling of laziness in there too. It's just easier to be like, "Well, the government said it. It takes too much time and resources to dig in whether the government is correct." So, there's a lot of issues going on.

Dr. Sam Dubé: There are. And you know what? The same thing is happening among physicians, where they are trusting of their governing bodies and not wanting to go further, sometimes not willing to go further because they don't want to look any further. And it's like, "Well, we'll just kind of, we have to have some faith in this organization. They give us guidelines." But then the whole idea that 2 big premises of medicine are do no harm and informed consent. Neither is happening right now.

Ivory: Oh yeah, informed consent really needs some improvement. I mean, I was assigned to cover COVID or COVID vaccines, but told, "Do not let people know about the thousands of deaths being reported by the CDC." The CDC on its website is saying, "This many people died after vaccination." We also got a few tips into the newsroom of healthy people who died immediately after vaccination. Like their families were letting us know these people died.

Dr. Sam Dubé: Wow.

Ivory: But because the main narrative was that, "The vaccines are safe and effective and will save lives," my bosses said, "Don't you dare say anything about these deaths to the viewers."

Dr. Sam Dubé: Wow.

Ivory: And that was very creepy to me and very unjournalistic.

Dr. Sam Dubé: My goodness, my goodness. You're dedicated to telling the truth. So, it looks like there's pressure financially. Here's the irony. So, you said this best yourself. You're like, okay, they first gave me the argument that, "People don't want to hear this," and you're like, "Which people? The people that don't want to hear the truth, or people that want to know the truth?"

Like people want to hear this, right? And then you said they're committing journalistic suicide. For the very reason you just expressed that people are going to question. If you're not giving them the information, helping them to decide for themselves, they're going to question. And that's what people are doing now. And this is why the Canadian Broadcasting Corporation issued their statement on the vaccines to reduce vaccine or just vaccine hesitancy. Because I don't particularly believe all the numbers about the percentage of people getting first dose and second dose. We know things. And you probably saw this in your creation of this story that's about to come out on Telegram, the PCR testing is extremely flawed. I don't know if you looked at that, the testing.

Ivory: No, I didn't cover that part. I didn't cover the testing.

Dr. Sam Dubé: Okay. So, this is definitely something you want to look into, the PCR testing. Even the inventor of the PCR test, Kary Mullis, the Nobel Prize winner, in 2019, he died shortly before COVID and under some interesting circumstances. But he had stated years prior, "You cannot use my test to diagnose an illness. You just can't. And this is well known, they went ahead and did it anyway. "Oh, yeah, there's tons of stuff here on the severity of COVID, but for the vast majority of people, it's a bad flu. But for the vulnerable, we need to protect them." And if you looked at the Great Barrington declaration that was created in Europe, it's been signed by tens of thousands of people, but 5000 physicians alone have signed this. Anyway, I'm rambling. I'm sorry. I'm rambling.

Ivory: No, that's all such intriguing stuff. But yeah, I mean, the news has just taken this vaccine narrative out of control. And the fact is that people are still catching COVID and catching bad strains of it, and even some people after vaccination. And most recently, when I talked to the Houston Health Authority about breakthrough COVID cases, the death rate for people who catch COVID after vaccination is the same as those who were not vaccinated. So, if you catch it, you have just as big a chance of dying. The news is not covering how to get better from a bad strain of COVID. What should you really be taking and where should you go? How should you really be treated? So, my report today is going to address some of that and some of the media narrative swerving around those facts.

Dr. Sam Dubé: Yes. And I noticed you interviewed Dr. Pierre Kory, who was part of the team under Paul Merrick, Dr. Paul Merrick there, who did the research. There's like 60 studies now on ivermectin. And another one just came out a couple days ago showing very conclusively that positive both as a prophylaxis and as a treatment. So, ivermectin is literally a cure here, right? It really is.

Ivory: That's what Pierre Kory says. Yeah. So, yeah, I'm kind of shedding some light on that research.

Dr. Sam Dubé: Thank God. Thank God. As I mentioned to you earlier, I did an interview with him in December of 2020, and his secretary told me I was the only one in the world that approached them on an interview after Senate address. And we went and we got shadow banned on YouTube. We got shadow banned on YouTube. We never made 5000 views. And here he was pouring out his heart about his research and about the senate address. And it was such a shame. So, we really need to shed some light on this, Ivory. And it's so wonderful that you're actually doing this and pursuing it. And you're pursuing it because you're pursuing it for the people and the truth. It's just so refreshing that there's still journalistic integrity in some people. Because, boy oh boy, I think most people, like just talking to people at the local grocery store when we're allowed to go, nobody trusts... we're still in lockdown where I am.

Ivory: Oh my gosh.

Dr. Sam Dubé: We're still in lockdown. Yeah, despite the beautiful weather and everything, and people are out there. The beaches are crowded, and public health is kind of like, "Oh, well, the numbers are dropping." Well, of course, the numbers are dropping. But if you look at the data on masking and lockdowns and social distancing, the real science is actually quite definite on what works and what doesn't work. So, what is next for you, Ivory, in terms of stories, in terms of career, in terms of maybe trying to look more at the truth?

Ivory: Well, once I get this COVID story out today, the next story I want to pursue is all these journalists I'm hearing from, I want to bring their voices forward and let it be known clearly I'm not just alone in this. I know April Moss already came out, and there's so many more. It's so sad that there are so many people who've been treated as journalists the way I have, and that the facts on the ground have been treated that way. So, I want to get that story out. I want to take a little breather. I haven't really had some peace in months.

Dr. Sam Dubé: No kidding.

Ivory: And then I want to continue doing journalism along with the other things that feed my soul, which are music and fitness.

Dr. Sam Dubé: Ah. Well, music I saw on your Instagram. You had that going as well. And fitness, maybe we have something in common there. And maybe we can discuss that another time. But can you give us a little bit of an inkling of what the predominant voices are saying among those journalists, what the feelings are, how they're coming to, what they're saying? If you can just give us a little preview of that.

Ivory: They were talking about suppression of stories. Quite a few of them talking about important stories that they had come across or questions the viewers had, and then the boss is saying, "Absolutely not. We're not putting that out. We're not going to allow answers to those questions." So, it's just very strange. It's like, "Why would you do that?"

Dr. Sam Dubé: Wow. So, really, a lot of reporters are caught in between. It's not like some big conspiracy where the reporters are like, "Well, let's lie."

Ivory: I'm sure there's plenty of bad apples among reporters. There are a lot of genuine, truth-seeking journalists who are caught between a rock and a hard place.

Dr. Sam Dubé: Wow. And, Ivory, now that I have you here, I wanted to ask you a little bit about the 2020 election, because you had mentioned you would receive some tips. Can you give us a little insight into what you think happened, and what the predominant view is from the non-mainstream media? What perhaps the view is from the ground with which you're very, very accustomed?

Ivory: Well, I think you wouldn't assume that every election would be spic and span perfect. There's the potential for anomalies and mistakes or fraud. If you really think openly about this, like it's pretty easily... you could expect problems to happen. So, the fact that Fox wanted to shut down any questioning of the perfection of the election was strange to me when I was getting details of things of concern. I was tipped off about the early vote count. Secretary of State's office of Texas was putting out raw spreadsheets of early voters who'd already cast their ballots in October. For the first time, you could just download the spreadsheets, go through all the names and voter IDs. It didn't say who they voted for, but you could kind of make sure everything was going smoothly. Compare those to the raw data from the voter registrar's website, which was transparent, and you could tell that there were many people who voted without voter ID. And when you check with the voter registrar, they do not show up as being registered to vote.

So, I came across a huge swath of people who were not registered to vote casting ballots anyways in Texas. And when I asked the Secretary of State's office about that, they weren't sure how that had happened too. I was like, "Is this a mistake in the counting? Or are people really getting away with not being registered?" They didn't have a clear answer. They were going to get back to me. They said they're forwarding it to the attorney general. I checked with the Attorney General too. So, here's the thing, they're like, "We're not going to have answers until like after canvassing," which was in December. So, I waited, kept checking back in. Canvassing came and went, and the votes were certified. They still don't have answers on that. I thought that was very strange.

And so, I pitched the story to my bosses multiple times, including when the votes were certified, and there was still no answer on these strange anomalies. And the bosses everytime acted like they didn't hear me. And so, it's just like, no, in fact, I think the first time I pitched it, they said, "Oh, I agree. We're going to forward you this study that came out that said mail-in voting is pretty, is foolproof, and when you study it, fraud does not happen. So, here's the study that said that. So, therefore, since it said that in the past, it can't happen in the future." So... No, okay, it was very strange. That was one of them.

There was then later in December, Harris County, the seat of Houston, it had to... the Commissioner's Court had to vote on new voting machines for the upcoming election. And it was the decision between 2 companies. And some of the county officials sent me a video of the one company demonstrating the machines and admitting to a fatal flaw where you can feed 1 ballot through multiple times and have it count for multiple votes. And the guy who works for the company said, "Yeah, sorry that that actually is a problem that could happen." So, theoretically, when the election judge is alone, they could grab ballots and start feeding them through multiple times. I was like, "Wow." So, that would be a public service to get this video of him admitting that flaw out to the public before the machines are voted on so we can make sure the machine with the flaw doesn't get voted on, if we care about election integrity. So, I pitch that to my bosses. They did not want to cover that. No interest, no interest whatsoever.

Dr. Sam Dubé: And there was something else you uncovered about Texas and the Dominion voting machines, and the decision that was made.

Ivory: Oh yeah. In November when Trump's legal team got together and did that big press conference talking about Dominion, they brought up Dominion for the first time, they mentioned Texas in that press conference. So, I was like, "Okay, there's a local angle. We can localize all this buzz about the election." So, I went and fact checked that, their statement about Texas. And sure enough, Secretary of State's office of Texas signed off on some legal paperwork back in January 2020 saying, "We will not have Dominion in our State. Dominion is not trustworthy." Texas Secretary of State sent investigators to look at Dominion machines closely in, I believe December, 2019. And they determined at that time, "These machines are prone to fraud, and we don't want them in our State." And the Secretary of State signed off in January 2020. So, that kind of proves there's something to these concerns about Dominion. Because before Dominion was politicized, Secretary of State's Office in Texas said, "Hey, we don't want to touch these."

So, Fox didn't want... they the bosses had no interest in that either. Yeah, that was the day they assigned me to a story of covering sidewalk chalk artists, which is pretty, pretty offensive that you would put me on a story about sidewalk chalk.

Dr. Sam Dubé: When this.

Ivory: When a lot of our viewers are very concerned about the election, and you are not interested in answering the viewers' questions about the election.

Dr. Sam Dubé: Oh, my goodness. That is just, it's unbelievable, and it's heartbreaking. Going back to your whistleblowing, Ivory, and this must be hard for you and your family and your friends. I know this was a long-time decision coming for you. And you thought about it long and hard. And it was a difficult situation to be in for those 10-plus months, at the very least. But what message would you give to other reporters right now? Looking at them right now, what can you say to them? Because you know them. You are them. What can you say?

Ivory: Well, America is hungry for some raw, real, authentic answers to their questions. There's a huge swath of the questions, and a swath of society that aren't getting answers to their questions. And if you are bold enough to just go seek those answers, you will put the pressure on your bosses. I mean, people need to just get some courage within the newsroom and go try to get answers to the stories. And if the bosses throw a fit about it, then record them. Let the public know. Your loyalty is to the citizens. And the truth is so important. And in an era when we're seeing such unprecedented things happen that make a lot of people afraid for the future of our country. Free societies are for, fortified by free speech, but if every journalist is timid, too timid to utilize free speech, then that could be the downfall of this society anyway.

Dr. Sam Dubé: Ivory, what do you say to a journalist that says, "But I don't want to threaten my livelihood. I don't want to I don't want to be fired. I don't want to get a reputation," what do you say? What do you say to that? I mean, these are very human concerns, right?

Ivory: Right. Yeah. And I was concerned about that as well. But look what happened to me. The country came rallying around me. And there's a giant market for some authentic truth-seeking reporters. And I think that America is ready to come support, you guys. And you can reach out to me and I'll shout you out and tell everyone else about you. And we can all be real, authentic reporters together.

Dr. Sam Dubé: Would you do that for Canadians as well? Because we have a real problem up here, Ivory.

Ivory: Oh yeah, any journalist around the world who wants to reunite their loyalty with the citizens rather than the establishment.

Dr. Sam Dubé: There is footage of a young reporter who is struggling to read a question in front of a microphone during an address, I believe, to some public health officials, possibly politicians. I can't recall which. The camera was on him, and he struggles twice to read this question. And he finally says, "Well, I'm just going to read the question the way it was given to me."

Ivory: Hmm.

Dr. Sam Dubé: Reporters here are being fed questions.

Ivory: Yeah. That doesn't surprise me after my experience this past year. So strange. They're like, "Oh, well only ask these questions." And I've been there in the editorial meetings when other reporters are saying, "Well, we need to ask the sheriff this," and the boss is saying, "Well, that question is just too confrontational for the sheriff. We need to protect our friendship with the sheriff. Don't you ask him that question." It's just not right. Public wants answers. [inaudible] public's questions.

Dr. Sam Dubé: We had a premier of Manitoba, Pallister, and he was asked a question by a reporter, very diplomatically, to consider ivermectin for treatment. This was a few weeks ago. And he shuffled some papers, looked down, took a long swig of his glass of water, looked right at the reporters or the camera or the audience and said, "We're going to try to get the vaccines made in Canada. It looks very promising." Completely not addressing the question about ivermectin. And then he thanked everyone, stood up and walked away. And the outcry was thundering to that.

Ivory: Wow.

Dr. Sam Dubé: What do you do to that? What can you do as a person or as a reporter?

Ivory: See, that's fantastic what just happened there. The reporter asked the people's question, and it absolutely exposed this guy. I mean, his answer right there is so telling. So that's all you have to do is ask the people's questions. It really doesn't matter how the public officials respond.

Dr. Sam Dubé: Okay. But then, I mentioned to you about the Canadian Broadcasting Corporation's vaccine hesitancy document, "No long-term side effects of the vaccine and spike protein is completely safe." To address this. How do we address that? I'm just asking. This is not to confront or corner you or any way. Like, I'm honestly asking, what can we do?

Ivory: People, journalists just need to return to their curiosity that they're supposed to have. You can't just take the government for its word. The citizens sure aren't. The citizens [inaudible] the government, and you've got to stick with the citizens. What are the citizens leery of, wanting answers to? Try to get answers. And something like that is a tricky one to go dig in and try to get answers yourself when nobody will verbally tell you the answers.

Dr. Sam Dubé: And as you were saying, the reporter in question with Pallister was actually voicing a question of the people. So, reporters, in a sense, are a voice for the people, correct? A voice for the people.

Ivory: Absolutely. I always think, "What would the citizens be asking if they were here? I need to be asking their questions."

Dr. Sam Dubé: Wow. I don't think... I can't say most, but... well, I could probably say most reporters are, think... I don't think most reporters are thinking that. I really... I'd love for them to think that. I'd love for them to think that. But I don't know. I don't know. I'm really looking forward to your story.

Ivory: Yeah, I've got to go finish that. I got another podcast coming actually.

Dr. Sam Dubé: No, and I realized that. And I want to thank you so much for joining us. Ivory Hecker, a journalist in the true sense of the word: a voice for the people. It was an honor to have you on our show, Ivory. Thank you so much. And hopefully, we can talk again sometime. Will you just stay on the line just for one moment and I'll sign off for us?

Ivory: Sure. Yeah, thanks for having me.

Dr. Sam Dubé: You're more than welcome. I'm Dr. Sam Dubé for the *Toronto Business Journal*. On behalf of all of us in the viewers, thank you, Ivory Hecker, for being a beacon of truth. And wish you all the best. And hope to hear from you again soon. And keep looking for the truth and we're going to follow you. Okay? Thanks.

Ivory: Alright. Thank you.

CPSIA information can be obtained
at www.ICGtesting.com
Printed in the USA
LVHW052319161121
703501LV00015B/330

9 781778 380013